The

Mouth

Trap

Strategies, Tips, and Secrets to Keep Your Foot Out of Your Mouth

Gary Seigel, Ph.D.

P CAREER
PRESS
The Career Press, Inc.
Franklin Lakes, NJ

THE MOUTH TRAP

EDITED BY KATE HENCHES

TYPESET BY MICHAEL FITZGIBBON

Cover design by Jeff Piasky

Printed in the U.S.A. by Book-mart Press

To order this title, please call toll-free 1-800-CAREER-1 (NJ and Canada: 201-848-0310) to order using VISA or MasterCard, or for further information on books from Career Press.

P CAREER PRESS

The Career Press, Inc., 3 Tice Road, PO Box 687,
Franklin Lakes, NJ 07417
www.careerpress.com

Library of Congress Cataloging-in-Publication Data

Seigel, Gary, 1950–

The mouth trap : strategies, tips, and secrets to keep your foot out of your mouth / by Gary Seigel.

p. cm.

Includes bibliographical references (p.   ) and index.

ISBN 978-1-56414-995-4

1. Business communication. 2. Interpersonal communication. I. Title.

HF5718.S438 2008

651.7'3—dc22

2007048045

Acknowledgments

I gratefully acknowledge the love and support from my family and friends. Special thanks to my three sons, Matt, Brandon, and Jordan, for their encouragement, and to Randi, who continues to be a best friend, mentor, and life line. Many thanks to David Vall-Lloveras, whose patience, computer savvy, logic, and analytical skills often create great balance to my sometimes chaotic travel life. Special thanks to Shoshona Brower, Lisa Valkanaar, Marty Reder, Brian Grossman, Ellen Kennedy, Gail Cohen, and the "elephant group" at National Seminars.

Thank you to my agent, Sammie Justesen, whose support from the very beginning made this book possible. I also extend special thanks to the staff at Career Press.

This book, though, would never have existed without the powerful experiences and tales shared by participants across the country in almost every city in the United States. I'm especially grateful to National Seminars, Aymee Martin at the City of Glendale, Scott and Leslie Seigel and their staff at California Closets, Mike Burke and the fine team at the Marine Maintenance Center, and the thousands of supervisors, managers, and employees whose stories inspired this book.

Contents

Preface

Once upon a time several hundred years ago in France, a king accused his prime minister and most trusted supporter, Pierre d'Pardoneau, of stealing gold from the royal treasury. The royal guards arrested him, put him in chains, and threw him in a dark dungeon. All night Pierre paced his cold cell, wondering how this could have happened. He figured the queen, an enemy of his for years, engineered the conspiracy and probably planned to replace Pierre with one of her people.

By morning, he could hear the sound of the blade sharpening down below, the scaffolding being built, and the guillotine slowly hauled from the office quarters to the outside court. He didn't want to lose his head, so Pierce knew he had to think fast.

That morning, the guards brought Pierre into the courtroom, in front of the King and a tribunal. An old judge stroked his beard and motioned for Pierre to come forward.

"Do you agree with these charges, my son?" the judge asked.

Pierre cleared his throat and somberly replied, "I do."

"You don't deny them?" the judge asked again, surprised.

The Mouth Trap

Though Pierre knew in his heart he had nothing to do with the stolen gold, he figured no one would believe him. Most prisoners protested their innocence, only to be declared guilty by the judge. In a matter of hours, they were executed. Pierre figured his only hope was to try a different tactic.

"I take full responsibility for the stolen treasury because I was in charge of the people who safeguarded the gold. I thought I chose people wisely. Apparently I did not. I am truly sorry."

The king scratched his head. He'd never heard anyone agree with the charges before or take responsibility for their own mistakes.

"Am I hearing you straight?" the king asked. "You're blaming yourself for something you didn't do?"

"Yes, your honor. I hired them. You trusted me to make smart hiring decisions, and I chose unwisely. I take the blame."

The king sat silent for several long minutes. No one in court said a word.

Finally, the king stood up and spoke:

"I cannot punish this man for a crime he didn't commit. He's been an excellent prime minister who has never given me any reason not to trust him. I will spare his life."

At that moment, the queen rose from her throne and raised her fists, protesting the decision, but the king silenced her. He turned to his advisors and royal officials, who watched with mouths agape. "Release Monsieur d'Pardoneau and let him return to his family!" the king announced.

As soon as the guards unlocked the handcuffs and chains that bound Pierre, dozens of journalists emerged from the crowd of spectators and barraged him with questions.

"So do you think the queen had something to do with your imprisonment?" someone shouted.

"Is there a conspiracy afoot?"

"Do you think the worst is over? What are you going to do, Monsieur, to protect yourself?"

Pierre knew that the conniving, German-born, and politically unpopular queen had been trying to get rid of him for years, so to have the king pardon him was quite a coup. He turned to the journalists and the crowd of people, raised his hands to quiet them, and then promised he'd make one statement. Raising his voice so that all could hear, he told them the following:

"I'd be an idiot if I didn't believe a certain foreigner wanted me out of the picture, but she's only a woman!"

(This drew tremendous applause and laughter.)

"And not even French, is she?"

The crowd applauded even louder.

"She's lost this particular battle," Pierre continued, "and if she knows what's good for her, she should watch her own neck!"

With this, the people stomped their feet and shouted Pierre's name. "d'Pardoneau! d'Pardoneau!" Now Pierre seemed inspired to speak even more. "And furthermore…" but his wife, who stood next to him, squeezed his hand, finally kicked him slightly with her foot, and managed to pull him off the stage.

As they made their way through the mob, Pierre's comments traveled from mouth to mouth, from journalist to peasant to the court officials, and by the time Pierre's words reached the King, the off-hand remarks morphed into a traitorous diatribe. "I don't know if you heard this, Sir," said one of the King's advisors, "but Monsieur d'Pardoneau called your wife a very stupid woman, a kraut, and a traitor who wishes to take over your job and our kingdom. He also said you would eventually chop her head off."

The king was furious. The veins in his neck bulged intensely as the words blasted from his mouth. "Bring Monsieur d'Pardoneau to my private chambers this instant!"

The Mouth Trap

Pierre could hear his own heart beating as he walked down the hallway toward the king's bedroom. He didn't believe he said anything that terrible. After all, it wasn't the first time the queen had become the center of controversy. *I'll apologize. I'll ask for forgiveness. He likes me. He's trusted me now for 15 years....*

Inside the king's chambers only the sound of the roaches scrambling across the wooden floor broke the eerie silence.

"Did you call my wife an idiot?" the king asked.

"No, of course not, Sir. Let me tell you what I said."

"And did you make disparaging remarks about her German heritage?"

"All I said was..."

"I also understand you think I'm going to execute her!"

"No, what I was trying to say..."

"What you were trying to say, you should have said in my office privately, many months ago where we could have discussed it—just you and me. Instead, you opened your mouth in public in front of people who all supported you and spread word through the town and the entire kingdom that I want to murder my own wife!"

"Your Excellency, I was only..."

In a matter of seconds the king ordered his guards to cut Pierre's tongue out and hang it on the door. His execution was scheduled for that same evening, and for weeks afterward, Pierre's head dangled—not on a stake outside the palace—but inside the actual court building, near the office supplies where all members of the court passed each day.

Many centuries later in the same building, Charles De Gaulle would pass the hallway and put his fingers to his lips to remind others to be watchful of the ghost of Monsieur d'Pardoneau who haunted the palace offices. And decades later, Presidents Jacque Chirac and Francois Mitterrand would reverentially pass the front hallway, never saying a word—a reminder to their staff that words can act like the sharp edge of a blade.

A small plaque with a poem was installed near where Pierre's head once hung. The poem is much better in French, but here is the translation.

Be careful of what we say
Such words across the land are sung
For those who think they speak one's mind
May end up losing thy precious tongue
The mouths can sputter, the words we utter
The outcome seldom falls into thy lap
For we must disclose what we've always known
Think first before falling into a trap.

Introduction

> *Remember our relationships are our keys to our-*
> *selves. How we treat others is how we will ultimately*
> *want to be treated.*
>
> *—Greesh C. Sharman*

Ever put your foot in your mouth? Have you at times kept your feelings in for a period of time and, instead of sharing them in a logical, persuasive format, you let loose and just exploded? Afterwards, you might try to explain("I can't believe I said that")or even apologize("Ooops. I am *so* sorry—please forgive me"), but the damage is done. You may repair the situation. You might restore your credibility, even your professional image, but, in the back of someone's mind, you are forever dubbed "the exploder."

And, of course, you'll be in good company.

As you read these words, a celebrity, a politician, a sports figure—perhaps even a well-known business executive—will be caught on tape throwing a tantrum, defending a DUI arrest, delivering a botched joke, or angrily grabbing a camera from a member of the paparazzi. Angry words of defense ripple across the newspapers of the world and stampede blogs, Websites, and news articles. Standup comics immortalize foot-in-the-mouth remarks, and cell phone cameras recount the incident via streaming video so millions of Americans can pass judgment on someone who, hours earlier, seemed to have a perfect life.

Who hasn't said the wrong thing at the wrong time and suffered the consequences? A sordid comment, a lie, or an irresistible truth told out of utter honesty—each can affect the way people see you and your team—perhaps the entire company. A politician who tells a bad joke embarrasses himself, his family, and his political party. When business professionals allow their emotions to get the better of them, people get scared! Employee morale drops. Customers don't call back. People quit or lose their jobs. The word is out: "Joe's a loose cannon," "Tom can't be trusted," "Phyllis went ape the other day."

It's human nature, though, to speak out. In fact, competitive, highly energetic, ambitious, goal-oriented people have the natural tendency to say what's on their mind and take risks. What do they have to lose? At the very worst, these direct, highly driven individuals will speak their truth, get in trouble, and beg for forgiveness afterwards. Unfortunately, knee jerk reactions and spontaneous verbal spouting prove irreparable. You can't take it back. People rarely forgive you, and they won't forget what you said. You may be a tough-as-nails negotiator, but if some racist comment or even just a sarcastic put down leaves your lips, you are forever remembered for what you said.

In the fable, Pierre holds important information in his head for weeks, maybe months, fearing that if he said something to the king regarding a conspiracy theory, he might be taking a big risk. *Do I speak up or not say a word? If I say nothing, I'm safe, but then I'm holding it in for a period of time, and who knows what I'll do! If I speak out, I might prevent a coup but will I be risking my position, even my life?*

Where do we draw the line?

Do I fight or take flight?

In a real office situation we don't fear losing our heads, but we may lose our jobs. To accuse someone of something as heinous as sabotage might be construed as paranoia. To bottle up emotions, however, letting them fester inside and eventually explode, is certainly not healthy either.

It's a real dilemma.

How do I communicate bad or less comforting news without releasing the "inner jerk" inside? And how do I say what I want without inciting the wrath of my "crazed" boss, who unravels every time something goes wrong?

In other words, how can we courageously say what we want to say without getting ourselves into deep trouble?

That is the focus of this book.

Just as we'll be examining ways to deliver tough messages that can be planned and thought out ahead of time, we'll also look at ways to avoid verbal eruptions and the damage they cause.

In the fable, Pierre ultimately sabotages himself by saying what he had been holding in for some time. Instead of courageously sharing his concern with the king, he rants: Feeling invulnerable, Pierre speaks words tainted with sarcasm and flippancy, saturated with anger. What might have been a tough-but-noble discussion has now turned into revenge.

To make matters worse, the words he said have traveled from the journalists, through the people, back to the palace.

17

Here's what he said: "I'd be an idiot if I didn't believe a certain foreigner wanted me out of the picture. But she's only a woman! ....And not even French, is she? She's lost this particular battle, and if she knows what's good for her, she should watch her own neck!"

What the king hears is quite different.

"He called your wife a really stupid woman, a kraut, and a traitor who wishes to take over your job and our kingdom. He also said you would eventually chop her head off."

How do we get from point A to point B?

Even hundreds of years ago, people played the telephone game. By the time a comment traveled from its source to its final destination, the meaning morphed. Pierre uses words that are open to interpretation. Though the populace might find this bold, funny, even courageous, the king and members of his court take great offence to its political implications.

Would you blame them?

It's bad enough that we express ourselves inappropriately, but to have it re-translated and re-invented (a normal process in most business environments), only magnifies and distorts the situation.

"Why that seems so unfair! My words were taken out of context."

"It was just a joke. Can't you take a joke?"

"That's not exactly what I said."

"My words were blown **way** out of proportion."

Centuries may have passed since d'Pardoneau spouted his passive-aggressive diatribe, but communication mistakes like that occur every day in the 21st century workplace. Some people blame it on a genetic problem—"bad wiring" installed in the brain that forces us to open mouth and insert foot. Others believe it's a personality trait they can't change or control.

And of course those of us eager to make more money and achieve our goals feel hampered by this crazy ability that we possess to rub human beings the wrong way.

The good news is that this behavior is fixable. Some who have higher levels of dominance and tend to be known for their bullying nature can learn to speak out and speak up courageously without relying on an automatic mechanism that immediately moves into blame, insults, and fury. In his book, *The No Asshole Rule*, Robert Sutton convincingly demonstrates how jerks in the office lower morale, increase absenteeism, expunge motivation, and challenge the psychological safety of fellow employees, all of which ultimately impact the financial stability of any organization. *The Mouth Trap* will show you how to create a healthy environment where conversations show respect and support.

For those of us who don't speak up, who fear confrontation, who just want to get along with others and not have to bring up unpleasant information that might irritate, frustrate, or anger a listener, we'll examine some techniques and strategies that will make difficult conversations easier and confrontation less intimidating.

After years of delivering tact and finesse workshops across the country—hearing as well as sharing embarrassing and often humiliating experiences of thousands of business professionals in nearly every industry—I have gathered the advice of experts and developed some guidelines that will help ease you out of seemingly impossible situations. Not only will you learn to take advantage of some secrets great communicators use to solve common problems and create rapport every time they speak, but you'll learn to take advantage of your own natural gifts. Throughout the book you will discover ways to improve your emotional intelligence, tap into your unique personality traits, and learn to become who you need to be so that you achieve the results you want.

The Mouth Trap

Included in every chapter is an action list, summarizing tips covered in the chapter that might help you think before you speak. You also have an opportunity to practice these steps by responding to a specific situation, and you can share your response on the *mouthtrap.com* Website. Discover other strategies and perhaps network with fellow business professionals eager to improve and become communication superstars.

Chapter One

Decide What You Want Before Opening Your Mouth

I don't let my mouth say nothin' my head can't stand.
—Louis Armstrong

While attending a convention, I met an old friend whom I had not seen in years. She gave me a hug and then stood back, smiled proudly, and pointed with her index finger to her waist line. She looked, indeed, like she had put on a few pounds.

"So when are you due?" I asked.

She straightened up, shook her head, and pointed this time more carefully to the badge hanging from a strap around her neck that dangled over her stomach.

"Gary, I wanted to show you the award I received. I've been inducted into the hall of fame. Isn't it gorgeous?" She paused. "And you didn't just ask me if I was pregnant, did you?"

The Mouth Trap

Whether we misunderstand or simply jump to conclusions too quickly, one of the most common ways we get in trouble is by simply speaking without thinking. Certain cultures, such as that of the Intuit Alaskan Indian tribes, have embedded into their linguistic structure a pause. It is natural to simply wait. Think it out. Then speak.

Some of the great communicators of our time know how to listen and respond carefully to what is asked. They choose their words wisely. Though it is sometimes frustrating that they don't always answer the questions, rarely will the successful ones say something they regret afterwards. They know the repercussions, and they take their time crafting what they want to say.

That's not always true for all of us. Our brain is divided in sectors that filter thoughts, and many of us who rely on our "gut instincts," who become accustomed to taking risks and instinctively speak from the "reptilian" part of the brain, will, most often, burst forth with whatever comes into our head.

Pierre d'Pardoneau held his feelings in for so long that when he finally had an audience that appreciated him, who applauded and stamped their feet every time he spoke, he released his innermost private thoughts. Unfortunately, even back then, words taken out of context took on an altogether different meaning. As I pointed out in the Introduction, by the time Pierre's address to the "people" made its way through the chatterbox/gossip pipeline, up to the palace, the words became decidedly anarchic.

Centuries later, messages not only become misinterpreted by simple word of mouth, but the media continues to transform or misinterpret what we say and do. Howard Dean's excited decla-ration of success to his fellow campaign workers in the 2004 election—"*YEEEEEEEEEEAAAAAAAR RRRRRGGHHHHHHHH*"—translated quite differently when audiences watched it on tele-vision across the country. What may have seemed enthusiastic and fervent to a "live" audience of supporters appeared manic, even insane, to millions of TV viewers.

Out in the parking lot of a large corporation in Anaheim, California, a bystander filmed a confrontation he witnessed and put it on *www.YouTube.com,* not realizing he had captured the barking, yelling, raving lunatic behavior of a fairly well-known vice president of one of the largest companies in the area. The VP was filmed chewing out an employee for parking in the wrong space. Though the VP later defended his behavior as inexcusable and an embarrassment, the moment will forever live on, especially in the minds of thousands of Orange County employees.

In the film *Love Actually,* Sarah (played by Laura Linney) finally manages to score a date with someone she admires. She's so excited by the prospects of having dinner with him, that when her date picks her up at her house, she asks him to stand outside for a moment while she goes inside, closes the door, and throws a tiny but therapeutic tizzy-fit.

Those are probably the kinds of out-of-control manic moments we could indulge in, don't you think?

Let's save any hostility for private moments when no one can hear or see us for not only does manic behavior make others feel unsafe, but it will haunt us and eventually cost us our reputations, if not our jobs.

One need only recall how fiery moments—even just a regrettable comment in the careers of the famous (Michael Richards, Russell Crowe, Mel Gibson, even Martha Stewart!)—cause careers to teeter-totter.

Jay Leno posed the ultimate question to Hugh Grant when he appeared on *The Tonight Show* many years ago after Grant had been arrested for "indecent conduct" with a prostitute. Leno asked, "What the hell were you thinking?"

It's a good question to keep in mind every time we want to open our mouths or do something without rationally thinking it out first.

More specifically, before we say something we regret, consider including four components that take seconds to answer:

1. Whom am I talking to?
2. What don't I know?
3. What outcome do I want?
4. What's the right thing to say?

Whom am I talking to?

If I'm speaking to someone who I don't know very well but who may be extremely important to my career, is it worth taking a chance and saying something that might have even the remotest possibility of causing trouble? It's this moment—this pause—this painful decision we have to make to say nothing. The infamous 20th-century philosopher Ludwig Wittgenstein wrote: "What we cannot speak about, we must pass over in silence."

Here's a recent scenario based on a real incident:

After hearing the title of my book, one of my son's friends, Joel, a 26-year-old film student who recently landed a hard-to-find internship with a well-known movie director, told me he needed some advice as he sadly shook his head. "I dropped a package at my boss's home. I had never been there before. It was a beautiful house in the hills, and when my boss answered the door, an attractive, seemingly older woman was standing next to him. Without thinking I said, You must be Bill's mom. What a pleasure to meet you.

"'This is my girlfriend, Sarah,' my boss told me, his eyes rolling so far back into his head, I thought he was having a catatonic fit. I not only made a stupefying mistake, but this was an internship I fought hard to get, and I figured he must think

I'm an idiot ready to be fired! And that's exactly what he thought. When I got back to the office the next morning, he left me a voice mail that basically said it was an honest mistake but if I ever did anything remotely dumb like that again to his family, friends, or clients, I would never work for him or anyone in Hollywood again. My career would be road kill."

Though we may have all been victims of what we might call "honest mistakes," people judge us on first impressions, and though in Joel's case, his boss may have dismissed the remark as coming from a kid who didn't know any better, this is not always what happens. Experts say it takes seven seconds to create an impression, and one second to destroy it.

What don't I know?

In the previous example, Joel could have either waited to be introduced or he could have asked, "How do you know my boss?"

In the earlier example about my friend pointing to her stomach, I could have merely asked, "What are you pointing to?"

This seems monstrously simple, doesn't it? Asking key questions positions ourselves quickly and easily to learn the facts before we make decisions. In fact, in any difficult conversation, you can avoid making false assumptions and generalizations by simply exploring first.

In the famous subway example Steven Covey gives in his book, *Seven Habits for Highly Effective People,* he talks about how he avoided saying the wrong thing at the wrong time by probing first. In Habit Five: "Seek first to understand, then to be understood," he describes a man with three noisy, screaming children who boards a subway and sits across from Covey. Instead of making the observation ("Why don't you control your noisy, obnoxious children?") Covey turns to the man and asks very simply, "What's going on?"

The father replies that he and his children just got back from the hospital where their mother died. "I don't know how to handle it, and I guess they don't either."

Now that Covey knows the context for the behavior, he can make the appropriate comment. "I'm so sorry you're going through that. I just want to make sure your kids are safe," would be more appropriate than making some judgment about his obnoxious children, especially at a time like this.

Probe first. Ask open ended questions. Get a sense of the "context" or the "lay of the land" before you speak.

Consider Jack's Story

After hearing from several people at work that his job may be in jeopardy, Jack stewed over the news for days.

Jack thinks, *I am so tired of the failure of this company to deal with issues straight on. I'm sick of the office politics. I'm sick of backstabbers. I'm tired of this boss who doesn't confront us but, instead, resorts to secret meetings, bad delegation, and acts of desperation. I can't stand it any more!*

One day Jack storms into his boss's office and without asking questions first, he says:

"I am hearing different things said about me behind my back, and I want to know the truth. Are you firing me or what? Because if you are, I'm going to file a lawsuit and it isn't going to be pretty. You understand?"

Seriously, who would walk into a boss's office and erupt in this manner?

Lots of people.

All across America, employees who fear confrontation and hold emotions back will explode like a well-shaken can of carbonated liquid. We call these people passive-aggressives, loose cannons, the out of control, crazy, wild people who used to work here!

Consider our options:

Do I say something or keep quiet?

In business, this is a familiar dichotomy. Either we speak or we withhold. Either way we create damage.

By saying nothing, Jack manages to internalize emotions that would eventually cause him to blow up. If he should bring up the rumors (private conversations he may have overheard), maybe he'd open a bag of worms. If what he heard was false, would sharing that information give the boss ideas and jeopardize his relationship with fellow workers?

If he does say something, how does he know the information he heard through the grapevine is even reliable? In an environment of trust, in which people expect to be told the truth and appreciate honesty and integrity, the choice might be easier. But in Jack's back-stabbing, winner-take-all environment, that may not happen.

Still, seeking clarification is the first step you take before you draw conclusions.

1. You confront the person who issued the rumor:

   "I just heard 'Jack's in for a surprise.' What does that mean?"

   or

2. You confront your boss.

   "I overheard someone say in the lunchroom, 'Jack's in for a surprise.' Perhaps I misread it, but would you know what that means?"

Before jumping to conclusions, find out what's going on. If it's true that your job's in jeopardy, then you have some options. Maybe there are misunderstandings or, at worst, areas you can change and improve so that you can keep your job. And if the rumors are false, what can you do to prevent the gossip?

So much of what goes on in business happens behind closed doors, filters through office politics, and becomes perpetuated. Ask questions to define the real problem before making the mistake of drawing false conclusions.

The Mouth Trap

What's going on?

Can you fill me in?

Anything you think I should know?

This is what I heard. Is that true?

Jack's dilemma is based on a real story from Irvine, California.

Here's what actually happened. After a day of self-torment and a night of sleeplessness, self-loathing, and paranoia, Jack approached his boss the next morning with an open-ended question.

Jack: Yesterday I heard some rumors that upset me. Is my job in jeopardy?

(The boss sits back in his chair, puts his arms behind his head, and smiles, as if to say, 'You caught me.')

Boss: We never received your report from last week. I'm told you were absent several days, and we're getting the impression, yes, that your heart's not in your work, Jack.

Jack: But I turned in the report last week to Fred. He didn't receive it?

Boss: No, Fred's no longer here.

Jack: It's been on his desk, then, for a week. I didn't know Fred left. Was I supposed to call him?

Boss: I can't believe it. (Meltdown!) *No, I delegated Ally to go through his stuff and get back to me. Wow! (Picks up the phone). Allison, would you come in my office please?*

If Jack had let it go right there, he probably could have kept his job. Instead, this is what he said:

*Jack: I can't believe that **you** thought I had just put the report off! What's the matter with **you!** This whole organization functions like it doesn't know its head from its ass! In fact, many of us are frustrated because **you** and others don't take the time to communicate*

clearly so that we can avoid stupid mistakes like this!
I can't believe how I've put up with this for so long!

Jack may not have planned to deal with the company's communication issues right here and now—his concern was his job—but in a matter of seconds he accused his boss of not knowing "his head from his ass" and of being stupid. In addition, the machine-gun repetition of the word "you" put the boss on the defensive.

If Jack decided at that moment to risk everything and lose his job, then he won the outcome he so desired.

If, however, he randomly shared these feelings and had all the intentions of keeping his job, then he made a big fat mistake. (Sometimes what angers us the most in others is the very flaw we "own" in ourselves.)

Jack was told to go home and "cool" off, but a week later, the boss sent him an e-mail giving him three options, none of which included keeping his job in the same city.

Would you want explosive Jack working for you?

What's my outcome?

In the formula, **E + R = O** (from Jack Canfield's The *Success Principles*), the **E** stands for Event, **R** stands for Response and the **O** stands for Outcome. Events happen, and it's our response to them that determines the resulting outcome.

1. Jack wants to burn his bridge and tell his boss off. That's one outcome.

2. Jack wants to keep his job, thank his boss for recognizing the problem, and perhaps see what he can do to help solve misunderstandings at work. Second outcome.

Obviously, these are two very different outcomes. Decide what you want before you have the conversation. Most of the time when we get revenge, it's not because we consciously created it—revenge seeps into our conversation like toxic wastewater. So if Jack wishes to address the communication issues, he needs to make clear ahead of time—in his head—what outcome he wants. We're assuming that would be an agreement between him and his boss to check with each other first before either of them draws false conclusions.

What's the right thing to say?

I often wondered how certain successful, smart visionaries can so brilliantly move their companies forward and yet make such decidedly bad choices when they open their mouths to speak. Obviously, when this abusive behavior goes unchecked, it continues. When the behavior creates great pain—financial loss, imprisonment, abandonment, grave illness—jerks re-think the way they talk with others.

Notice in the next example how easily Martin could have avoided a terrible mistake that affected not only him personally but the financial safety of his company:

> *Martin, a sales manager, was helping customers in the showroom of a custom shutter company when he heard his salespeople in the hall laughing and making noise. He poked his head into the hallway and told his salespeople to "stop the socializing. Can't you see I'm out here helping a customer!" and resumed his conversation with the client.*

That's all he did.

The salespeople were actually celebrating the closing of a $10,000 job. Martin didn't know that. He also didn't realize that these salespeople were not so fond of his snapping at them. So when they went back to their office, they stopped talking about business and instead gossiped about Mr. Snap Turtle. To make matters worse, when one of the installers, Bill, wanted to meet with Martin that afternoon, Bill was told by the salespeople not to see Snap Turtle because he was in a bad mood. Not only did

Martin not get the information that he needed from the installer, but he never heard from his customer again except via e-mail:

"I've decided to use another company. Thank you very much."

Martin's quick reaction ("Stop the socializing") ricocheted throughout the company, alienating salespeople, his installer, and customer, costing him and the shutter company perhaps thousands of dollars.

What could he have done differently?

Scenario:

> **Martin:** *Hey guys! What's going on?*
>
> **Salespeople:** *We're celebrating. You won't believe the big job Trudy just closed.*
>
> **Martin:** *Fantastic. Could you keep it down or move back into your office? I'm trying to set up another appointment for one of you, and it's a bit noisy.*

Everything we say generates a response or a reaction. Martin decides he wants to find out why his salespeople are so noisy, so he probes. He tells them what's in it for them—an appointment means money! And in seconds, he gets what he wants.

> *"HR managers estimated that costs...time and dollars spent related to [a jerk's] treatment of people totaled about $160,000."*
> —Robert Sutton

Those five seconds of damaging knee-jerk emotion may not cost Martin six figures, but if you calculate the time apologizing, regaining his credibility and commitment, not to mention the loss of revenue when he loses a potential customer, that can mount up. Saying the right response will reverse this trend and help Martin achieve exactly what he wants: happy salespeople, more customers, and bigger profits.

Let's say, however, Martin wants two things. He wants quiet, **and** he wants to teach his salespeople a lesson.

How dare they—don't they know better—I can't believe they're talking right outside the showroom! Are they nuts?

Separate the Issues

When we want more than one outcome, we muddy the waters. This is not to say that Martin can't achieve all his outcomes, but he may not want to go after them all at the same time. He can deal with them separately.

At the time of the incident, he could ask for what wants. Here it is slightly rephrased:

Martin: What's going on, guys?

Salesperson: Oh we're having a little celebration here. Tammy just closed a big builder for $10,000 worth of shutters.

Martin: Congrats. Great! I'm trying to help a customer here, and set up an appointment for one of you. Could you keep it down?

Then later on, after the customer has left, he could say to them privately:

Martin: I was irritated earlier because the noise in the hallway made it difficult to hear and converse with a customer. In the future, could we keep the hallway free of noise because it's so close to the showroom?

If Martin wants to discuss the "noise" factor and set a policy, he can do that separately, at the right time, in the right place. The salespeople are celebrating an awesome sale. Don't burst the bubble. Acknowledge their success.

Trick #1: Recognize, acknowledge, and support at the beginning of a "difficult" message. Most people want to feel appreciated. Rarely will you find an employee who will come home from a job complaining, "I am just being recognized far too much! I can't stand all the wonderful attention!" Instead, people often feel so unappreciated, so misunderstood, that when they're told what to do, they react negatively.

Trick #2: Martin includes a reason: "Could you keep it down? I'm trying to set up an appointment for one of you with the customer." That's it. Reasons are your gift to your fellow staff members or employees to let them know why you want something done a certain way. If they don't know why, they'll ask others to clarify the situation. If you give them the reason in a way they'd appreciate, you're more likely to get the outcome you want faster.

Every minute of the day in every work environment, employees ask, "Why should I do this?" That frustration makes them feel de-valued and unimportant. Hunting for a key reason and sharing it with the employee can demystify one's job and create an environment that inspires productivity.

Trick #3: Separate the issues. Don't speak to them all at once. If "noise" in the hallway may be an issue, treat it separately when the customers not around, avoiding phrases like, "You irritated me," or "You made so much noise in the hallway." Rely on "I" statements like "I felt irritated because of the noise in the showroom." "I'd like to make certain in the future that discussions take place outside the hallways so that customers don't hear the noise." You can also ask the question: "Have you guys ever noticed how the noise in the hallway carries into the showroom?"

Devil's Advocate*: Okay, Dr. Gary. My reptilian brain works on overtime, and when I get angry and all huffy, I just can't think logically so meditating over "What's in it for my listener" and "What outcome do I want" is way out of my league. I mean if my* *salespeople are rude, talking in the hallway, I'm going to tell them to shut up—end of story. And if I have a colleague at work that is bugging me, I just say it like it is. One of my favorite phrases? "Get out of my frickin' face!"*

Dr. Gary: *You're absolutely right. We do let our reptilian brain—our animal instincts—tell us what to do. This part of the brain, by the way, says "I'm hungry. Feed me," or "I have to go to the bathroom now!" or, "I want sex immediately!" There are appropriate and inappropriate times to follow these urges, and my suggestion is avoid being reptilian during conversations. Take a breather. Move out of that side of your brain (right side) and realize your emotional response could be dead wrong. Ask and probe first to get the big picture. Like a detective, you will gather your information first before making a decision. If that doesn't help, re-think all the times you followed your "urgent" need to reply, and how often did you spend hours, days, maybe weeks, cleaning up the mess? There are many different ways of doing the same thing. You may want to teach someone a lesson, but find the right way to do it.*

Action Steps

Making the decision to speak or not to speak is not always easy. Should I bring this up? Maybe I should just let it be. I'm not sure how they're going to take this. What if I get in trouble? Here are some action steps to consider that will help you with this process:

1. Who is your listener? You'll speak differently depending on the age, gender, job title, and relationship you have with that person.
2. Remember the beer commercial that coined the phrase, "What's up?" Ask questions. Research

issues. Find out as much as you can before you draw conclusions. Probe first.

3. In the formula E + R = O, you probably have no or little control over the event. That's the situation or problem with which you're dealing. You can, however, choose your outcome. Envision what you want and that will help you create the proper response.

4. Prioritize these outcomes. If you can't get all that you want in one conversation, separate the issues. When Jack goes to his boss to discuss a rumor, he may want to solve that first and choose the right time to discuss rumor control in the office.

5. In addition to these four steps, consider acknowledging the listener's pain and offer explanations that will show the listeners what's in it for them.

And now I have a question for you...

The following true story deals with a difficult encounter with a customer service representative. How would you have handled it?

The Case of the Rattled Rental Car Agent

After flying from Anchorage to Seattle, Reynaldo rented a car and started driving to his destination in the state of Washington, nearly two hours from the airport. As he was driving, he realized that the interior reeked of cigarette smoke, and he knew two hours of smelling smoke would make him sick, so he turned around and drove back into the rental car lot.

As he trudged up the steps with suitcases in tow and approached the service desk, the rental car agent seemed engrossed in a "heated" conversation.

"Alice—no. I have the kids this weekend. Yes, it's my weekend—*not yours*! Hold on a second." The agent put the phone on the desk and turned to Reynaldo. "Yeah?" he asked.

The Mouth Trap

Reynaldo pointed to the keys he placed on the Plexiglas surface and took a deep breath.

"This car smells of smoke," he told the agent. "I'd like another one."

The agent's face, fraught with life's torments, stared at the car keys and looked up at Reynaldo as if he were going to spit.

"This," the agent said, holding the keys in his hand, and putting an accent on each syllable, "is a non-smoking car."

Yeah the car may not be smoking but the guy in it was, Reynaldo wanted to say, but he remembered the advice his grandfather once taught him about not getting hooked into other people's troubles: Reynaldo counted to 10 and took a long, deep pause.

"Look," he finally said. "I have breathing problems, and this car smells of thick cigarette smoke. Could you find me another one, and I'll be out of your office in no time. You can finish your phone call."

But before Reynaldo could finish his sentence, the agent's cell phone rang again, and he was now back on line with Alice, cursing and yelling.

"Alice, I don't know. I have this guy here. Yeah, at one in the morning he's lucky to have any car at all. Hold on a second!" (He looked at Reynaldo) "Mac, there's nothing else I can do for you."

Short of ramming his fist down the agent's throat, Reynaldo could barely hold his cool at 1 a.m., but he somehow handled the situation quite calmly and within a minute or so, the agent handed him a set of keys to a Mercedes equipped with Satellite Radio and a GPS system.

What do you think Reynaldo did to get more than the outcome he desired?

(The actual solution, by the way, is found later in the book in Chapter 11.)

Chapter Two

Don't Listen to the Voices in Your Head

> It is hard to fight an enemy who has outposts in your head.
>
> *—Sally Kempton*
>
> If your mind is empty, it is always ready for anything; it is open to everything.
>
> *—Shunryu Suzuki*

Joe sits in the lobby of an office, waiting for an important job interview. He pretends to read a magazine, but from the corner of his eyes, he checks out the other applicants in the room, sizing them up. Their shoes are shinier than his, their teeth whiter, their hair darker. Even the clothes they wear look newer and more expensive. Joe remembers the sandwich he ate at lunch contained garlic, so he digs for the last Tic-Tac in the bottom of his brief case, only to find it stuck to the plastic lining. *Great,* he thinks. *I not only look bad, I smell awful, and I'm totally disorganized.*

At one point, the secretary pokes her head in and chats with a couple of the candidates as if they were old friends. Joe overhears phrases, like "You're the best" and "Why, that's perfect!" Though he hasn't a clue about the context of what's been said, he *assumes* these people already work for the company, and they have an "in" he does not have. Just as he looks at his watch, figuring he hasn't a chance in hell of landing this job, the secretary calls his name.

You're going down! a voice in Joe's head says, as he trudges into the boss's office.

The boss, perhaps tired from a morning of interviewing, sits slumped in his chair, and immediately Joe thinks, *He doesn't even want to talk to me. I am wasting my time. I may as well make this short and sweet. Get out quickly and move on to another job interview because this is a total disaster.*

You Are Your Thoughts

There is no reality. There is only perceived reality.
—Tom Peters

What Joe perceives—an uninvited, disinterested office environment—may not be reality. Like Joe, we often take what we see around us and make up an elaborate fantasy world that we think is true. At the same time, Joe creates a perceived reality. If his tone of voice remains listless, his shoulders slumped, his eyes staring at the floor and his arms crossed, the secretary and the boss may think, *What a loser. What's he doing here?*

So when Joe walks into the boss's office, he listens to the voices inside his head. These thoughts become the only message he hears, and they sabotage his delivery. Even if Joe has what it takes—the skills, the top resume, the recommendations—he believes he doesn't have a chance, and it is that belief, written all over his body and inscribed into his soul, that the boss sees and hears.

Self-sabotage

You are your thoughts. The thoughts in your head are what institute the laws of attraction. You think therefore you are.
—Joe Vitalli, *The Laws of Attraction*

We have a choice: We can let defeat get to us and imagine the worst, or send our brains a clear, positive thought, signaling the path to success. It costs nothing to take the more positive approach, but for some of us, we are drawn to the dark side. This is a hopeless situation, our thoughts tell us. Why bother?

In one of my workshops, I assign a drawing exercise. It begins like this:

1. I ask everyone to find a partner. I have them sit directly across from each other so Partner A can see the power point on the screen and Partner B cannot.

2. I give the following directions: Partner A is to get Partner B to draw exactly what is on the screen. **Rule #1:** You cannot cheat. In other words, Partner B cannot turn around and look at the screen, but Partner A can describe the picture as vividly as possible, offer feedback, and answer any of Partner B's questions. **Rule #2:** Do not cheat. Do not draw for Partner B. Just give clear directions.

Usually the drawing is a series of geometric shapes, and nearly every group in every workshop completes the assignment accurately in less than five minutes. However, during the first 30 seconds after giving directions, I always hear expressions of embarrassment, humiliation, and shame:

"Drawing? Are you kidding? I'm terrible at drawing."

"Oh, my God! Let's switch seats. You're better at drawing than I am."

"No, I'm not good at giving directions, you are!"

39

The Mouth Trap

"You've got to be kidding. My drawing skills suck!"

Remember—this exercise is usually completed accurately by 95 percent of those who attempt it. Still, most people THINK negative thoughts that suggest this task is too challenging.

"I'm going to embarrass myself by drawing" or "I'm going to be inept at giving directions."

versus

"I am listening. I am following directions. I am capable of making this work."

I carefully watch the groups that avoid self-sabotage, and they are the ones who do the exercise faster and finish first. This is the believability factor. If you believe it will happen, it will happen, so believe in the outcome you most want.

Let's go back to Joe. He's waiting in the lobby for the interview, and he says to himself, "I'm great at interviews. I'm practicing. I am in that position behind the desk with the window. I'm in control."

If Joe wants that job badly enough so he can enjoy the pleasure of great pay and a prestigious position, he will fight for it, and his self-talk will reflect that attitude. Or, to avoid the pain of rejection and the fear of losing the job, Joe can talk himself out of it, excuse himself, or blow the interview by simply going through the motions.

Anthony Robbins points out that everything we do is influenced by our need to avoid pain or our desire to gain pleasure. "If you develop the absolute sense of certainty that powerful beliefs provide, then you can get yourself to accomplish virtually anything." This includes things others believe are impossible.

You don't have a chance. Those others are so much better than you. Get outta there!

versus

I have as good a chance as anyone. I'm great, awesome, unbelievable. I can't wait to prove myself.

It is a simple turn of the phrase.

The problem is, of course, we are often better at talking ourselves out of something than we are at talking ourselves into what we really want. Once we make a decision, however, that *moment* must be clear, directed, and focused.

Living in the Moment

In the movie *Jerry Maguire,* Tom Cruise plays the title character, an outgoing, energetic sports agent, who is fired from his job after he shares his mission to infuse honesty and integrity into the business. Now on his own, he must sell himself and persuade athletes to hire him for representation. At first he attempts to sign a number of clients from his previous employment, but he fails every time. Without a shred of success behind him, he gradually wins the favor of Rod Tidwell. Played by Cuba Gooding Jr. (who won an Academy Award for this part), Tidwell motivates Jerry to repeat the phrase— *Show me the money!*—over and over again, like a parrot channeling a Wall Street tycoon. "Show me the money!" Jerry screams repeatedly, louder and louder, the words transforming and inspiring him, giving Jerry the necessary confidence to succeed. He must, if nothing else, live in the moment.

Up to that point, Jerry seemed desperately distracted by his mission statements and newfound idealism. Once he focuses on what his clients want—They want money!—and not on what they view as less important—four-star hotels, front-page coverage on a magazine—he can close the deal.

The question we can always ask ourselves may be a familiar one:

What is this about?

Is it about my desire to show off? Or is it about getting my clients the money they want? The more selective we are, the easier it is to visualize what we want. If there's ever a time to be "in the moment," to set our sights on the goal, it is before a job interview, or before a difficult or crucial conversation.

Living in the moment is a decision we make before we speak, before we tell a joke, or respond to an interviewer's question. If we're functioning out of desperation and fear, we'll probably say the wrong thing (and often regret it afterwards).

"You know, this job's not for me. I can't believe you kept me waiting an entire hour in that room!"

"I guess this is going to be bad news, huh! I'm an idiot for putting up with this."

If you've ever interviewed people who seem addicted to their negative thoughts (Cherie Scott-Carter calls these folks "negaholics"), you can hear the despair, anger, doubt, and sense of doom in their speech and see it in their body language; they slouch, hold their heads down, and refuse to maintain eye contact.

If only the candidate would consider an alternative: Take a few minutes before the interview, close the eyes, and think: *Okay, what outcome do I want and how will I create that? How do I have to look and what am I going to say to get what I want?*

Ever pump yourself up?

Here is what I want! I am focused. I am here to get this job. That's my goal. Nothing is going to get in my way.

Joe envisioned himself as a badly clothed, stinky, yellow-toothed alien in a gray pin-stripe world. *No one's going to hire me,* he figures, and he's right. Since he talked himself out of the interview, he could, if he had the right sensibility, talk himself into it. He has that choice.

Getting Coached

When Brandon took his oral exams for his Ph.D. in history at Rutgers, he felt poorly prepared. He thought he knew certain historical events better than other events and believed he could strategize and maneuver topics into more familiar territory if necessary. He was a high achiever who won awards and maintained an A average all through graduate school. But the night before the test, he had dinner with one of his friends, a brilliant student in the same program, who confessed he'd failed the oral exams twice before finally passing them.

"You did what?" Brandon asked. "You're the top student in the class. You received your BA and Master's from Harvard. How did you fail it twice?"

"It's frickin' hard, man," Mr. Harvard replied.

Brandon came home a jittery mess. If Harvard Man failed the orals—twice—then how would he—a mere state college graduate—pass? *I don't have a chance!!*

He shared these fears with his wife. She encouraged him, but apparently to no avail, for he barely slept the night before the exam and awakened the next morning pale and sick to his stomach, too nervous to take the test.

"I'm going to bomb. I know I am," he told his wife.

"No, that's not going to happen," his wife replied.

"I barely slept! I can't think! I'm screwed!"

The Mouth Trap

That morning, Brandon's wife decided to become his personal coach. She put on a Rocky Balboa t-shirt and forced Brandon to do a series of calisthenics, then personal "I" statements (*I am in the moment, I am doing great on this exam*), more pushups, and then more affirmation statements (*I am an expert on 18th century British history*) until he felt focused.

"Is this about Mr. Harvard or about you?" she shouted.

"It's about me."

"I can't hear you!"

"It's about me!"

"And what about you?"

"I am fully capable of passing this test. I am a brilliant strategist."

"What was that?"

"I'm going to pass this exam!"

"I'm sorry. I can't hear you. Give me 15 more!"

"*I am a brilliant strategist!* I've studied for 10 years. I am passing this exam!"

(Quite different than the "stuff" in his head the previous night: *I don't know what I'm doing. This sucks! I can't remember anything. I don't belong in the same category as Harvard guy. What am I going to do?*)

Brandon entered the oral exam feeling invigorated and alive. He gave the performance of his life. He did not know every question. In fact, a whole section on 18th century satire stumped him for a bit, but after the exam, the three faculty members commented on the confidence he showed, the depth of research and knowledge he displayed in certain areas, and his ability to pool from other events and historical moments. His attitude more than made up for his inability to answer a couple of literature questions.

Attitude isn't important...it's everything

When we deal with challenges, we either talk ourselves *in* or talk ourselves *out* of decisions. Take your pick. Our heads fill with thoughts that reflect the philosophies of both camps, and it's sometimes hard to differentiate between the two voices.

The Coaches vs. the Dementors

Football teams have coaches—sometimes specialty coaches—who inspire and motivate players minutes before they run onto the field. "You guys together? We're going to wipe them off the face of the Earth! What do you say?"

If a football player is having a bad day—failed a test, lost a girlfriend, experienced a tragedy, got sued—coaches motivate them to get into the moment and think only about the game. Once on the field, cheerleaders continue to "cheer" the players with elaborate rhymes and rhythms. The day's excitement is often built on the complex gymnastics routines that inspire the players to be their best. Signs above the games, an organ player in the distance, and huge electric billboards encourage the crowds to cheer and stand on their feet. This, we hope, energizes team members so they'll win.

Imagine now, if we had the opposite—instead of cheering our sports figures, we imported the "dementors" from the *Harry Potter* series, these dark cloaked demons, who, in my version of the story, heckle the players and remind them of how badly they played in the past. "You're the worst! Get off the field!" the dementors scream. These rowdy spectators sit in the stands, jeer at the players, and share their commentaries (and obscenities) out loud in order to intimidate all the team players.

In our heads, we hear similar voices:

"You're a terrible salesman. You can't even close half your leads."

"What an awful parent you are."

"You can't pass that test, you dummy!"

Every word the dementors use knocks us down a notch.

"You're not getting that raise! Those other candidates are way ahead of you!"

We can hear voices that demoralize us ("You are worthless") or we can choose to hear the voices that invigorate and inspire. ("Man, you're the best. Go for it. Don't let anything stand in your way!")

I did an experiment at my office when I was in the closet-remodeling business. I had half my salespeople listen to the radio (the stock market, soaring unemployment, the causalities of war, and Middle East horrors). I also told them it was all right to talk on the cell phone with family and friends on their way to jobs. Ex-husband didn't send the alimony? It's fine to deal with that before you meet with a client. "Listen to whatever you want before you start your day. All's fair."

I told the other half of the sales force to listen to only motivational speakers, and I gave them specific disks, even sections of disks I felt were particularly invigorating.

I also told them they could not, under any circumstances except in an emergency, take or accept cell phone calls from family or friends.

Do not check thy personal voice mails before going to a client's house.

Leave the alimony issues, the unpaid bills, and the fear of World War III at home.

Your job is to live in the moment and sell closets.

Guess which group did a better job?

No surprise here.

Group B's closing rate was nearly double that of Group A's.

In fact, Group B made twice the amount of money as Group A. This was not a scientific test. The results were not consistent, and I'll admit certain salespeople in Group B would have done better no matter what. But Group B let the empowered messages inspire them, and they brought *that* inspiration with them on the sales calls.

You can listen to bad news and to your partner's litany of bad news before going to work. Alternatively, you could reframe your thoughts so when you enter your work environment, you've created the moment that will get you the outcome you want.

Press the Delete Button

Try writing down some of the thoughts you have about the people you work with and the clients you service.

Are you allowing these thoughts to seep into your conversation and speech patterns? If this "dementor" language is sabotaging the way you engage with others, delete it from your head. Get rid of it!

Tips to Help You Achieve Clarity

Tip #1: Take a break, clear your head, and visualize the outcome.

"Sally, I'm going to step outside for a moment. Can you call me when it's my turn to go into the interview room?"

"John? I need a couple of minutes to walk outside and think this through. I'll be right back."

Tip #2: Taking a breather is an obvious alternative to speaking too soon, especially in emotional situations.

If you know what you want and you know what you don't want, you can seek the language that will get you there. Yet, you hear dementor language creep into people's speech every day.

The Mouth Trap

How many times have you heard a speaker get up and say, "You know, I didn't have much time to prepare, and I'm not much of a public speaker, but…."

(If you tell me you're not prepared, I'll believe it. Get off the stage!)

"Jack, I'm not an idiot."

(Whoever said you were? But now that you mention it, maybe you are an idiot.)

"I can't believe I'm even saying this."

(Then don't say it!)

"I probably shouldn't be saying this. I don't know why I'm even talking to you."

(Stop wasting my time!)

The brain, this intricate computer capable of processing up to 30 billion bits of information per second, listens to what we think. If you *think* you're going to blow an exam, you will most often create what the brain tells you to create. It will manifest itself in the way you *feel* (sick, lost, sinking feeling) and then create a *behavior* to match (you flub your lines, forget your facts, fail to synthesize information).

Thoughts Create Feelings. Feelings Create the Behavior.

I am prepared. I am a great scholar. I am loved and adored. (That's the thought.)

I feel confident and capable. (That's the feeling.)

I am answering the questions. I am making clear connections. My ability to remember quotes is stellar. (That's the behavior.)

If you often speak without thinking, look for the thought.

The thought is what drives the feelings and the behavior.

Consider this example:

Ever hear someone say, "That's going to make me sick" or "You're going to be the death of me?" A friend of mine told me about a high school teacher who fell into the habit of complaining to his family and friends about his students. He'd whine and holler that kids today weren't the same as they were years ago. He'd roll his eyes, shake his head, and while putting his hand to his heart, moan, "They're killing me!" At first, my friend said he thought the phrase was funny, because it imitated a popular commercial for mattresses in which the accountant pleaded with the owner of the company to stop slashing prices. Apparently, though, the teacher's wife grew tired (and embarrassed) by her husband's dramatic display and told him to stop it.

She spoke too late.

The teacher's brain was so used to hearing the "killing me" message that these very negative thoughts finally kicked in on the day of his retirement party: That day on the tennis court, he dropped dead of a heart attack.

Did his words kill him?

Of course not. He died of coronary thrombosis.

Still, the thought—*these kids are killing me*—may have led to feelings of *inadequacy and weakness*—which could certainly contribute to the deterioration of heart muscle.

Far fetched?

The way our bodies behave is greatly influenced by the thoughts and feelings inside our heads. Dr. Norman Cousins, writer, philosopher, and literature professor said, "Just as there is no loss of basic energy in the universe, so no thought or action is without its effects, present or ultimate, seen or unseen, felt or unfelt."

If we tell the body enough times how unhappy and miserable we are, the body listens. Words have a power of their own to instill feelings (inadequacy, weakness) and inspire

49

behavior (errors, mistakes, failure). If we can reframe the thoughts, we are much more likely to create the kind of actions and behavior we want.

In Brian Tracy's *The Psychology of Achievement*, he reveals how the brain physically reacts to negative messaging. In fact, he cites studies that show how negative thoughts actually reshape the cavity in the brain and affect the way we speak, talk, act, and walk.

If you know any negative people at work, you can hear it in their speech patterns, in the way they hold their heads and the movement of their arms. We see people at work who seem discouraged, disgruntled, and miserable, and we comment on it: "Had a bad night, Joe?" "What are you worried about?" "What's the matter?"

When we're sad, we cry. When we're embarrassed, we turn red. If we get nervous, we shake our leg, or talk too quickly, or sweat. Thoughts have a remarkable effect on our bodies.

In one scene in the New Age/metaphysical documentary entitled *What the Bleep Do We Know?*, a monk blesses a drop of water, and the water takes a round shape. When teenagers yell at the water, it takes an oblong shape. Because our bodies are made up of more than 75 percent water, our thoughts can physically affect the shape of the water. So when someone yells at us, what happens? We feel uncomfortable, nauseous, perhaps just plain sick!

The night I saw this documentary with my friend Ellen, we were in Portland, Oregon. Driving back from the theatre via one way streets, we got lost, and I blamed Ellen for not going to Mapquest or Google and getting accurate directions. In fact, I was so frustrated with the maze of streets and the time it was taking to find our hotel that I finally yelled at her: "Ellen, I can't believe you didn't get accurate directions this afternoon. What were you doing all day for God's sake? This is just so crazy. We won't get back until after midnight, and I have to get up early, and do you know what it's like to function with five hours of sleep instead of...." And I went on and on, blaming her for the long ride home.

Once my tirade ended, Ellen grew quite sullen and she said, quietly: "Gary, that hurts my water."

On the one hand, we do not want to inflict our "gunk" on other people. It hurts their water! Language has a clear, physical effect we can often witness by simply looking into the listener's face. That's why I appreciate live conversations versus e-mail. At least when we face someone, we can see the reaction and respond accordingly.

Now imagine this same language embedded into our consciousness. We yell at ourselves. We talk ourselves out of performing well at interviews or at meetings. We import dementors that change the emotional chemistry of our bodies. If Brandon managed to let Harvard Man get to him, he would have flunked the oral exam and his life might have been very different. Imagine if Abraham Lincoln had convinced himself not to run for president after he lost eight elections and suffered a nervous breakdown. Or if a young Austrian body builder with a thick accent let the naysayers—movie critics, columnists, and journalists—talk him out of becoming not only the number-1 box office star for a decade, but the governor of California! Had Thomas Edison allowed dementors to infiltrate his mind during his thousand or so failed experiments with the light bulb, how much longer would the world have been sitting in the dark?

Anchoring

"I am driving safely and getting home quickly. I am following the map perfectly."

Affirmations are not only the better way to go, they're the only way to go before you open your mouth.

Step 1: Affirmations

Maxwell Maltz describes affirmations as an "automatic creative mechanism" that can initiate real, positive, goal-oriented results. "Once you give it a definite goal to achieve, you can depend upon its automatic guidance system to take you to that goal much better than 'you' ever could by conscious thought. 'You' supply the goal by thinking in terms of end results. Your automatic mechanism then supplies the means whereby..." (*Getting Things Done*, David Allen).

We subconsciously do what the brain tells us to do. You just have to set it up. When Maltz says, "You supply the goal by thinking in terms of end results," you would simply create, in your head, the outcome you desire.

I am in this job.

I am winning this customer.

I am inside that interview room giving the interview of my life.

These are positive, personal, and present tense affirmations that set the goals in action.

Use "I" statements, not "you" statements.

I am having a great interview, not *You are having a great interview*.

Use positive words. Avoid any negative words like *not, don't, shouldn't, never, couldn't, however, yet, etc.*

I answer all the questions intelligently, not *Do not blow the questions with stupid comments*.

Speak in present tense.

I am meeting with Jack today and we are closing this deal, not *I will be meeting with Jack today and closing the deal*.

Step 2: Create Visualizations

David Allen, organizational guru, says, "You won't see how to do it until you see yourself doing it," so let's examine this particular component. Remember Joe—the young man who talked himself out of a job while waiting for an interview?

Imagine if he visualized a different reality. Instead of the miserable, negative, indifferent world he perceived, Joe imagined rapport and agreement. The boss nods, takes notes, and verbally shows approval. The secretary talks to everyone in the room. I'm a superstar, Joe says, knowing full well he has what it takes.

> *Mere thought can alter physical structure.*
> —Merton

Walking on Hot Coals

I experienced the most powerful example of visualization while attending a "Warrior" workshop in Santa Barbara, California, back in the mid-1990s. After many intensive days of exploring our personal goals and intentions, we were asked to participate in one last exercise. Our facilitator had arranged for hot coals to be placed across a long grassy area, and we were encouraged to use all our positive self-talk and imaging to create the thoughts that would allow us to walk successfully across hot coals barefoot.

For some, this was a simple decision. A friend said, "You got to be kidding. I'm going to burn my feet. I'm going to spend the rest of the night in the hospital!"

For me, it was a slam dunk. I visualized the opposite. I saw myself walking across the coals, burn free. And I didn't just visualize it—I played the role. I became a coal walker.

I am a coal walker. I am burn free.

I visualized myself walking across the coals (like the other coal walkers), feeling proud and responsible. I didn't see myself screaming "Oh my God, I'm on fire!"

(You might laugh, but some people did think that!)

I was married at the time, and my wife, Randi, wanted to walk the coals with me, but she said she wasn't ready. The assistants had just raked the coals so they were bright red, and she wanted to wait.

I was fully ready right then, and I wasn't willing to wait. Reluctantly, Randi joined me on the fire walk.

As we stood on the edge of the coals, I did my self talk. In fact, I sang in my head *burn free* to the tune, "Born Free." I psyched myself into being fully ready.

I am a coal walker and with the warm *coals under my feet, I feel impervious to pain.*

I didn't burn my feet.

Randi, on the other hand, got slightly burned, and to this day she often speaks of that experience as a moment of realization: Instinctively, she knew she was not fully ready, but she felt caught in the illusion that she was prepared, and so she walked the coals anyway.

Step 3: Act the Part

My thought: *I am burn-free. I'm a coal walker.*

Randi's thought? *I am walking the coals because my husband wants me to, but I am not fully ready.*

The outcomes were very different, so as a result of this experience, we learned to approach a difficult task or situation by "checking in" first. What's our level of confidence? Am I prepared? What am I worried about? What do I need to do and who do I need to become when I have to deal with a difficult situation?

In *Jerry Maguire*, we see the main character pump himself up, put his hands over his face, breathe deeply, and become who he needs to be (a dynamic salesperson) before he walks in the door of a particular client.

Sarah Myers McGinty, in her book *Power Talk*, states that "acting like you know what you're doing can contribute to your success." If you walk into a meeting, knowing full well that you will face a confrontation, assume the role that gets you the outcome you desire. *I am here to create agreement: a win-win for both of us. I am walking into that meeting fully focused and charged.*

Joe Learns the Lesson

It's now 1 p.m. Joe is home after the interview, and the secretary calls to tell him he didn't get the job. As much as Joe tries to remember his positive self-talk, he succumbs to the dementors and falls into a sea of self-pity, misery, and depression. He is so consumed by the bad news that he thinks he may never ever find a job again.

It's now 1:05. The boss calls back and says, "Ooops, my secretary made a mistake. She was reading from the wrong paper. We hired you. We want you, Joe."

Joe asks, "What's that again?"

"We want you, Joe!" the boss repeats.

Instantly, Joe's water returns to its normal temperature. He smiles and grows calm as his thoughts re-group and recover. The tears disappear. The heart no long sinks to the pit of his stomach, and he can now feel his pulse beat at a normal rhythm, feel the blood surging, the adrenaline rising. "Oh, my God!" he shouts. "I got the job. I can't believe it!"

Nothing actually physically changed to create this—only a few words: "Oops" and "We hired you." Four magical words transformed Joe's mood from the miserable to the excited.

That's it! Joe realizes at this very moment that he has control over what he thinks and how he feels—an amazing realization. If those words ("We want you") can inflate his spirits and "You didn't get the job" deflates them, he can put the words into his head that will get him the results (or insults) he wants, every time.

Before a challenging or difficult conversation, center yourself with your thoughts, get "into the moment," and use affirmations and visualizations. We fall into the Mouth TRAP when we let negative thoughts sabotage the outcomes we desire.

Action Steps

Here are some immediate Action Steps that will change the way you think so you get the outcome you want every time.

1. Avoid prefaces, introductions, and excuses that frame your talk. Enter a conversation with the impression you want to create, not the impression you don't want to create. You can train yourself to do this by making it a habit. "The way to make better decisions is to make more of them. Repetition is the mother of skill," says Tony Robbins.

2. Choose your words wisely. Pick language you would choose as part of mission statements: affirmative, personal, and positive. Avoid dementor language, the language of defeat.

3. Visualize what you want and announce it out loud. Believe it. State it. Ask for it.

   "John, I know we have a tough project to work on, and I'm planning on giving you an 11 out of 10 performance, so you let me know if I'm living up to that expectation. Okay?"

4. If the previous approach is too bold, try this one: Ask for a progress report. You can say, "My goal is to lead you guys to success so that we see the profits rise, get bonuses at the end of the year, and work together as a team. How am I doing?"

5. Infuse yourself with positive self-talk. Don't overwhelm yourself or else you'll become like that

Stewart Smalley character on *Saturday Night Live* ("By George, I like myself"). But self talk can be a powerful tool that can make the difference between success and failure.

6. Find a mentor who displays these positive attributes. I will admit certain radio shock jocks I like to listen to are not motivational before going on sales calls. Turn the radio off. Find the right voices (either on CD, DVD, or on radio) and listen to those.

7. Disengage from those who get to you emotionally. Just unhook or stay away from them.

8. Make a habit of *thinking* first. Make certain the feelings these thoughts create are positive and present tense, and then visualize the behavior you'll exhibit.

And now I have a question for you...

Marjorie: "I was working with the VP of Operations at a large software firm and we were creating a health and life insurance program that would be available to every administrator and employee in all divisions. It was a big deal, and as I came closer to landing the account, I grew weary of the VP's questioning, probing, and obsession with detail. I finally said, with anger in my voice, 'Obviously, you think I don't know what I'm doing, Jules. I do. I've been doing my job for 15 years!'

"There was a long silence. The VP said he'd call me back, but he never did. In fact, he never returned any of my phone calls, and I heard through the grapevine that he found me 'incorrigible.' I called. I wrote an apologetic e-mail, and then a letter. I never heard from him. As a result, I lost not only his business (4800 employees) but that of his network of friends— a $.5-million mistake?"

The Mouth Trap

Chances are, the client dropped Marjorie because of a series of issues, but her statement—"Obviously, you think I don't know what I'm doing..."—was the catalyst that convinced the client to give up on her.

What could Marjorie have said differently? How could she state her point and yet earn the outcome she so desires? What "mind set" could she create in her head before she opens her mouth?

Chapter Three
Death by Conversation
(Tips and Strategies for Becoming Better Listeners)

> *Everything has been said before, but since nobody listens, we have to keep going back and beginning all over again.*
>
> —*Andre Gide*

"So what do you do?" I ask the man sitting next to me on the airplane.

"I'm a geophysicist" he said, gleefully. And he went on to describe what he did and how, where, why, who, when, and where he did it. His words sounded like this: crwoworor rock and mmsmedmemgmma salination plants and ltltlehwllele tldlslshsh thththeheisowoe slshgfotyt wowod kxkfhgh no water for California..."

Had I not been clueless about physics and the other scientific information he shared with me, I might have been interested, but he lost me inside his first sentence. By the time our plane left the ground, I wanted to punch him.

The Mouth Trap

Reader, confess: Have you ever been forced to listen to someone who just won't stop talking? The blather goes on and on! We feel like that woman from Airplane! *who turns into a skeleton after listening to the person next to her talk nonstop. I asked myself:*

Should I tell him to shut up?

Should I pretend to listen?

Can I interrupt without seeming rude?

What should I do? I don't want death by conversation!

If we feign interest, the speaker thinks everything's fine and continues talking. That's one option.

"Wow. Yeah. That's cool. Wow. Okay." I keep nodding, pretending to follow the endless train of thought, and ultimately feel helpless and trapped.

Or I could say it like it is: "I don't have a clue what you're talking about. What you're saying is boring the living daylights out of me, Jack. Either change the subject, or I'm moving my seat."

(Nah, that isn't good. As mouth trap graduates, we know better than to resort to rudeness. And besides, the plane was full.)

Here's a better option:

Gary: I don't have a clue about geo-physics, but I'd love to hear what you do. So tell me—what impact will your work have on me living in Los Angeles? (He laughs, pauses, but starts all over again. Yikes! I have to stop him before it's too late.)

Gary: You don't understand. I can't follow you. I was an English major and never took a physics class in my life. Can you tell me in one sentence the impact your research will have on my life over the next— let's say—20 years? That way I'll be able to follow more clearly what you do. (I look at my stopwatch.)

You have 30 seconds. (The man pauses again and smiles. I think he gets it now. He closes his eyes, pinches his temples, thinks again, and speaks.)

Geophysicist: *I try to make sure you'll have water to drink 50 years from now, though I'm concerned that may not happen.*

Gary: *But what about the oceans? Can't we take the salt out of the water?*

Geophysicist: *Absolutely. They're doing it in various countries particularly in the Mediterranean and the....*

Gary: *Just tell me the countries.*

Geophysicist: *Saudi Arabia and Venice, Italy.*

Gary: *Thank you. So why only there?*

Geophysicist: *It's very expensive.*

Gary: *How expensive?*

Geophysicist: *Well, let...there are lslslslsll fhththehe sosososo thththehe sososo—*

Gary: *No! No, just one word. Please.*

Geophysicist: *Billions.*

Gary: *Thank you. So are we in some trouble here?*

Geophysicist: *Where do you live?*

Gary: *Los Angeles.*

Geophysicist: *That's right. I guess I wasn't listening. Well, that's putting it...let me explain...you see—*

Gary: *Oops! Answer me yes or no. Are we in trouble? That's all I want to know.*

Geophysicist: *Yes. Big trouble.*

Gary: *I want to hear more. Let me buy you a drink with one of my Southwest coupons.*

Geophysicist: *We're on United.*

Gary: *Details, my friend.*

I'm not suggesting you have a conversation like the one I just described. Coaching a stranger on how to speak may not be appropriate, but if you asked me what I'd want to hear from a perfect stranger speaking on an unfamiliar topic, I'd say, "Make it memorable." Bullet point it for me. State it simply and let me ask questions. Don't deliver a soliloquy unless you're James Earl Jones.

Intrigue me. Cater to your listener. Use core words and core messages. Astonish me. Sum up your point of view. Pitch your ideas; don't let them get entangled in phrases, clauses, and complex sentences. If we expect people to hear and appreciate what we say, make it engaging!

So let's look at listening from two perspectives:

1. What can we do to make our listeners truly listen so they not only remember what we say, but pay attention to *everything* we share?

2. What responsibility do we have for hearing and listening to what is sometimes impossible gibberish?

Creating Messages That Grab the Listener's Attention

What is this compulsion some people have to tell *everything* that's going on? If I were a physicist, Mr. Geophysicist would probably grab me from the moment he said "borehole measurements." I'd be right with him. I'd ask questions. In fact, I'd live with him inside his words and complicated ideas. But I'm not a physicist and "borehole measurements" means nothing without some context. Better to make it memorable.

Here are six ideas for how to make any presentation "stickier" from *Make it Stick* by Chip and Dan Heath.

1. Keep it simple.
2. Include the unexpected.
3. Use concrete words and images.
4. Make it credible.
5. Incorporate emotion.
6. Use little miniature stories.

The geophysicist could have said:

"I help communities find healthy drinking water so they can survive in a world where healthy drinking water is scarce. In fact, we may run out of water in our lifetime." Those two sentences cover a lot of ground. It's **simple**. Water is scarce. Then he adds the **unexpected**. "WE could run out of water...seriously!"

Water is a **concrete** topic because anyone can understand and relate to "shortage of water."

The man is also **credible** because he's a geophysicist. And his news is **emotional** because I worry about surviving without water. To drive home his message, he might include a **story** about how difficult it is to find water. In fact, one fascinating story about his trip to Saudi Arabia to visit water conversion plants might have made his message truly come to life.

Creating memorable messages means turning our thoughts and feelings into spoken words that a listener can understand and appreciate. That is not easy. Here's one version:

"Amplitude variation with offset (AVO), borehole geophysics and rock properties, coupled by the use of ground-penetrating radar have made it possible for geophysicists like me to unearth and discover ground propensities that prove the scarcity of water."

Here's another version:

"We're going to run out of water."

The Mouth Trap

Which statement do you like best? Of course, the second one is much more concise, but depending on your audience, (that is, a roomful of geophysicists), the first version might be acceptable. In either case, listeners in today's marketplace will tune out the message within the first few minutes if they can't find the meaning.

The movie business, in fact, can teach us an important lesson in regards to core messaging. In Hollywood, most writers must "pitch" an idea before a producer or executive will consider even reading the script let alone funding it. If you're lucky to address a room filled with movie executives, you might have one minute to state your idea. Many a movie won its funding based purely on a carefully crafted pitch.

Let that be a metaphor for the conversations most people want these days. Sure, it's fun to sit down with Grandpa and reminisce for hours, meandering in and out of real and fictional memories. This kind of listening, however, hardly exists in business—especially among the younger generation who grew up on fast food, video games, MTV, sound bites, and, now, streaming video. If *Gone with the Wind* were made today, instead of an elaborate party scene lasting nearly 40 minutes, the film would begin with a battle scene. Someone would die, and within five minutes of the opening credits, the Civil War would begin.

Here's a quick summary of some tips for creating core messages that inspire good listening skills:

> ➢ Hook the listener.
> ➢ Synthesize your information and just give them the meat.
> ➢ Create the bottom line.
> ➢ Tell them what you want them to do and how you want them to do it.
> ➢ Don't make people translate your thoughts into *their* language. Make your message compelling and memorable using words they'll understand.

In fact, if you speak my language, then I'll listen. This is not merely a choice, by the way. Our brains actually react or respond to specific messages. When experts let the "curse of knowledge" take over their speech, and speak too long or in too technical a language, the listener's brain shuts down. Physiologically, the brain can only capture information it can process, and if the brain can't digest or synthesize the words, then the thoughts move elsewhere.

Let's see. I wonder what we're having for dinner tonight. Now that's important.

Netherlander account? What's he talking about? Isn't USC playing this Saturday?

We search for meaning, and when there is none, we move on.

Like a computer, the brain simply turns off when it cannot digest what it hears or when it perceives information as old news. I've heard this before. I'll wait until I hear something new. Shutting down!

The brain also shuts down because the listener is indifferent to the material:

- ➢ We simply don't care. The subject doesn't interest us.
- ➢ We're rehearsing what we're going to say next.
- ➢ We have other things on our minds that take greater priority.
- ➢ We misinterpret language based on past experience. "No" can mean "maybe." "Someday" might mean "never." "It's not up to me ask your father" might mean, "Not a chance in hell."
- ➢ We not only misinterpret but re-interpret and synthesize based on an elaborate series of defense mechanisms. If we think the speaker doesn't like us or differs politically from our perspective, we tune him out.

> We'll read into things that don't exist. (What water shortage? That's a big political plot to Greenpeace the world!)
> And if the speaker placates us—"This may be a little bit over your head"—our ears perk up, we roll our hands into fists, and our adrenalin kicks in.

There must be a better way.

Here's a case study that shows the power of partnership listening where both parties take 100-percent responsibility for what they say and what they hear. From my perspective, this is the only type of communication we should have at work and at home, but we let so many distractions get in our way.

Though most of the examples in this book are work related, I've chosen a case study based on a personal relationship. Sometimes we listen differently at work than we do at home, and here's an example of that.

Meet the Yardleys

Every year, John and Barbara celebrate their anniversary with their friends Jeannie and Al at El Nido, one of their favorite Mexican restaurants in Ensenada, Mexico. They usually drive down for the weekend and stay at one of the posh resorts. As they're clicking wine glasses and eating delicious Mexican food, Barbara brings Jeannie and Al up to speed about a redecorating project to re-do her entire bathroom.

As Barbara describes in detail the materials they chose, her husband, John, drifts off, thinking about his business (he's a scientist for NASA). Though he still remains at that table, he could have easily been sitting on the moon, for he doesn't hear a word his wife said.

"And I've been asking John what colors he wants in the bathroom but I haven't received a straight answer yet...John? Hello, John, you there?"

"I'm here."

John nods and smiles, having just returned to planet Earth.

"What are you thinking about, hon?"

"I'm sitting right here. I'm listening."

"What did I just say?

"You were talking about the beach...."

The other three laugh and shake their heads.

"He's so cute when he lies, isn't he?" Barbara exclaims. "That was 10 minutes ago, sweetheart." Barbara leans toward her husband and pinches his cheek.

"Ouch! That hurt!"

Good friends for decades, they laugh and joke about John's ability to zone out. Al even slaps him on the back at one point and exclaims, "Hey, man I have to tell you—you're great! I wish I could zone out like you when my kids are chattering like magpies in the backseat of the car."

All seemingly goes well until John and Barbara return to their hotel room that night.

Barbara sits on the edge of the bed and says, "John, I have something to say, and I've been meaning to say this for some time. I hate it when you tune me out like that! It's embarrassing and rude. The kids have commented on it because you do it with them too. My father has said numerous times—'Where's John?' when you're sitting across from him at the dinner table. I worry you'll pull the same stunt at work and get fired."

"That will never happen," John said.

"Why not?"

"Because I pay attention there." He sighed. "Please don't take this the wrong way but Barb, I just don't have any interest in what color toilet we install in the bathroom. End of story. Now are we going to make love or what?"

Barbara sits back and takes a long, deep breath. Her husband had earned a Ph.D. in astronomy. He was a Rhodes

Scholar and the author of two textbooks. He spent years working for NASA, Rockwell, and Boeing. But he didn't seem to know a damn thing about being a good listener and a good husband.

"Do you think this discussion is about a toilet?" she asks, finally.

"Isn't that what you're upset about?"

"No. It's about the fact that you remember what you want to remember, but you forget what's not important to you."

"I fade out for a few minutes during what was essentially a boring conversation, and you have a cow?"

"Boring for you, I agree. Not boring for us. When you speak about your bowling leagues at work, or a particular tough day refiguring a jet-fueled engine, I do my best to listen. I do. It's important for our relationship. I force myself to pay attention because I love you, and I want you to know I'm interested, even when it's a struggle to understand what you're saying. The fact that you only listen to what interests you is selfish. I feel undervalued. I won't tolerate this behavior any longer and it's going to have to change, right now, or this vacation will be eternally on hold. Now you can either sleep on the couch over there, or you can put that rocket-scientist brain to work and tell me what you're going to do differently. Is that clear? "

John feels dumb-founded. He sits on the couch, scratching his balding head, and tells his wife he is willing to do almost anything but sleep on what he dubbed "this ergonomic disaster!" She smiles, pats the pillow next to her, and says, "Then, let's talk."

Barbara's Perspective

Can you blame Barbara for being upset? Not only does she feel discounted and unimportant, but she can't get her husband of 25 years to admit (let alone recognize) he tunes her out whenever it's convenient for him.

She feels she goes out of her way to listen when he comes home from work, but that trait is not reciprocated. Why not, she wonders? He could at least recognize this difficulty and work to improve it.

In fact, she would like John to incorporate a lot of new techniques into his listening skills:

1. Ask questions. If the subject doesn't interest him, guide the speaker into a different direction.

2. Admit the truth. "Barbara, I really don't want to talk about the bathroom. Can we switch topics?"

3. Acknowledge the listener's desires. In this case, she'd like to be listened to.

4. Whatever is on your mind, stake it. If you're thinking of other things—take a moment and write it down, remove it from your head, and listen.

5. Reflect on what's been said. "So what you're saying is that the bathroom will take four weeks, and you have it all designed, but you still need a few more bids. Right?"

6. Validate. "I think that's a great idea."

7. Sometimes we have relationships with people, and we have to bite the bullet and show interest. Use eye contact. Be present.

8. Paraphrase. Put what they said in your own words. That process keeps you awake and makes you part of the conversation.

John's Perspective

John is bored out of his mind! Years ago he tolerated these evenings but lately, he's been so involved in his work, that few topics interest him. We know how hard it is to pay attention to a conversation we don't care about, so what could Barbara have done to grab John's attention?

The Mouth Trap

1. Customize the conversation

Scenario One:

Barbara: "John, remember that heated toilet seat we saw at Phyllis's house last week? Pretty amazing, huh?

John: Oh my, my, my. That was amazing. We tried installing one of these on Pluto II but we ended up spending the money on an air conditioner instead.

Scenario Two:

Barbara: John—John? Tell Al what excites you about the new bathroom.

John: You got to be kidding. Nothing!

Barbara: Oh, come on! What's the one thing we've been doing that you liked?

John: I can't think.

Barbara: And what bothers you the most on cold mornings when you get out of the shower?

John: Oh, that! I hate the cold floor. We actually found a device that will heat the floor instantaneously so when you get up in the morning and it's 10 below outside...this thing is amazing...it blah blah blah...

2. Make the message memorable

If Barbara could customize the topic for John, that would draw him into the discussion. She could make it possible for him to not only relate to the subject, but to address it with authority, in his own techno-speak language. If she had done that—used the **concrete images** (heated floor/heated toilet seat), spoke to a particular **emotion** (excitement), and worked within his **expertise** (he loves gadgets!)—the conversation would have been far more successful.

As partners, John and Barbara can become honest listeners. If the conversation truly doesn't interest John, he can say, "Listen guys. I can talk about the bathroom remodeling job for a few minutes but if we're going to spend the whole evening on it, that's going to be painful for me. Would 15 minutes be enough?"

Such honesty may not always be possible at work, but as partners, you and your boss, or you and a fellow employee, have numerous options to choose from to make a conversation work. If, however, you simply can't concentrate—You've tried to "stake" the information, you've taken notes, you've nodded, you've stood up, you've validated and nothing's working. You feel yourself drifting into never land—what do you do?

You could raise your hand, and say, "What you're saying is important, and I want to listen, but right now I have so many things on my mind that I am just not able to concentrate. Could we reschedule this for later today? How about 4:20?" Or if the subject is simply irrelevant to your expertise, "I'm having a hard time following you because I have no background in this area. Let's see who does so that you can get your questions answered."

Everything Changes When We Use the Telephone

Because so much "listening" is done on the phone these days, let's examine some of the traps we fall into when we're conversing by wireless or via land lines.

The Deadly Phone Call

Bill's in the Philadelphia office: 8:43 a.m. EST.

Frank's on vacation in Maui: 2:43 a.m. Hawaiian Time.

Frank: (Quite groggy) Hello?

Bill: Frank, I'm having a problem here with the software.

71

The Mouth Trap

Frank: What?

Bill: I said I'm having a problem with software. The password works but information gets automatically (The phone cuts off. Bill calls back but the line's busy. He calls again.)

Frank: Have you any idea what time it is, for God's sake?

Bill: I've gone through a number of tests. I talked to Alex but he can't figure it out.

(Crying baby in the background. We hear Frank's wife's voice in the background, shouting,"Who's that? For God sakes, we just got the baby back to sleep!")

Frank: Just figure it out. Ask someone else. I won't be back in town until late Wednesday. (Frank hangs up.)

End of phone call.

Ever receive a phone call in the middle of the night or at a bad time, and you obviously don't feel like talking? At two o'clock in the morning, Frank will not be receptive. As a consequence, neither Frank nor Bill will listen for important details, so, because the "timing" is off, this conversation proves disastrous for both parties. Bill feels hopeless because a software problem will impair customer service. Frank lies awake until morning, worrying about problems at the office and listening to the baby scream. And to make matters worse, Bill believes Frank will be at work on Wednesday, although Frank made it clear he won't be back until late Wednesday night.

Even the phone itself—with its pauses, mysterious glitches, and lost calls—makes it difficult to hear and understand all the information. As a result, Bill can't get the software to work. The customer goes elsewhere. Angry at Frank for not helping, Bill storms out of the office the next day, declaring,"Everyone takes vacations but me!" and fires off an e-mail demanding time off.

The situation explodes into a disaster.

Three things could have been done differently that would have enhanced partnership listening:

1. Acknowledge each other's feelings before dealing with facts.

If Bill recognized he awakened Frank, he could have started the conversation with an apology, given Frank a reason for the early morning call, and established rapport.

The rule is in situations like this: Feelings first, then facts.

"Frank, I am so sorry to awaken you. I wish I could have waited but I have an impending disaster in my hands, and I could use your help."

Ideally, he would wait until a reasonable hour and make the call based on Frank's time zone. Chances are, if Bill didn't disturb Frank sleep, he wouldn't hang up, the baby wouldn't awaken, and problems would be solved. Instead, both men disengaged.

2. Speak in concrete terms.

Because the phrase "late Wednesday night" is nebulous, Frank could have avoided that glitch by being more definite: "My plane gets in at midnight on Wednesday, so the earliest I can be in your office is Thursday at 9 a.m. Is that clear?"

Or Bill could repeat back what he thinks he heard and check for misunderstanding. If you think, however, any of this is going to happen at 2:43 a.m., you're dreaming. Both listeners had attention deficits. Each man closed his mind to the truth because emotions consumed their thoughts. In a one-on-one conversation, the other party's body language tells you right away whether or not this is a good time to speak, but on the phone, this can be a challenge. One of my favorite phrases when I begin a phone conversation is to ask: "Is this a good time?" "Do you have a moment?" If the moment's bad, the conversation's not going anywhere.

3. Make that listener your partner.

So if Bill were savvy to Frank's situation—it's 2:43 a.m.—he has a baby—and on a second honeymoon in Maui—might he have had a different conversation?

I would think so.

And if Bill were savvy to Frank's problem—probed and found out the real issues and deadlines—might he have been more empathetic?

Move from an adversarial approach to a partnership, taking full responsibility for what you say and what you hear, and you'll reap major benefits.

Ideally, human resource managers want to hire good communicators who have impeccable listening skills. Here's a sample "help wanted" ad:

Wanted: Professional Listener

➤ Must have knowledge of reflective listening, body language and attentiveness, excellent tone, and good summary/paraphrase skills.

➤ Nodding preferred.

➤ Knowledge of listeners—inside/out—mandatory.

➤ Please, no broken record, zoning out, or placating.

➤ Must have excellent cell phone skills and the ability to read into/between the lines. Subscription to a no-lost-calls cellular service a must.

➤ People with "attitude" need not apply.

➤ Ability to slow down when leaving your phone number.

➤ Good core-message/story telling skills a must, and the ability to take 100% responsibility.

➤ Special attention to dates, times, deadlines, and numbers are imperative.

➤ Salary: $1 million.

If you ask human resource managers the magic ingredient great job candidates should possess, listening is always near the top of the list. This vital skill can be learned, practiced, toned, exercised, and developed, but if we're hard-wired to zone out, interrupt, judge, misinterpret, and disengage, listening can be a big challenge.

⌐ Action Steps ⌐

1. Make your communications memorable by focusing on the core message.
2. Use concrete nouns and adjectives the listener can understand and appreciate.
3. Customize your message to the listener, keeping in mind job position, personality, gender, and age.
4. Listen with heart and soul. Take notes. Make sure it's a good time. Stake information that may get in the way of listening. Reflect back on what's said by "checking in" with the speaker.
5. If you like the idea of creating a partnership with your listener—whether it's on a phone or in person—visualize the outcome. Focus on what you have to do to create a clear direction.

And now I have a question for you...

In an interview with Gina Piccalo for the *Los Angeles Times*, actor Jason Schwartzman (*Rushmore, The Darjeeling Limited*) prefaced his remarks by saying, "My feelings won't be hurt if you cut me off. I can be slightly long-winded." That's okay, perhaps, for an interview with an actor who is in Piccalo's words, in the "white-hot center of young arty Hollywood." But what happens when we encounter this in everyday business? How do we deal with long-windedness?

Chapter Four

The Personality Chapter: Know Your Audience

> *How do other people experience me? Am I respected? Am I seen as a jerk? Who am I in their eyes?*
>
> —*Philistina Markowitz*
>
> *A person's speaking style and 'tone of voice' can predict objective outcomes with 75- to 85-percent accuracy.*
>
> —*Robert Sutton*

Knowing Your Audience

Joel, the manager for an electronic firm, gave an award dinner for his staff. After the meal, he embarrassed Mary, a software security engineer, by calling her up to the podium to give a speech. The shy 30-year-old had been recognized for her excellent work that year, but she pleaded with Joel to just let her say "thank you." Giving speeches wasn't her thing, she told him, and when Joel coaxed her on, asking the entire roomful of guests to encourage her to speak, shy Mary finally stood up in front of 250 people, nervously stumbled over her words, and barely uttered a few sentences before she finally sat down, quite embarrassed by her inadequate performance.

Joel's wife elbowed him afterwards and told him that was a really stupid thing to do.

"What? What did I do?" he asked.

The next day Mary called in sick and confided with several of the employees that she was so humiliated, she was afraid to ever show her face at the office again. They assured her she did just fine, but the staff agreed: Joel should have known better than to force an employee to get in front of a roomful of strangers and give a speech.

But Joel found the reaction from his employees puzzling. "I don't understand why everyone's so damn sensitive!" Joel confided in his secretary. "I certainly don't see how I offended Mary. I pointed out how she's improved during the past year and gave her an award! The woman wouldn't even give a little speech, for God's sake!"

"That's because you're clueless," his secretary told him. "You embarrassed her by asking her to give a speech when she wasn't prepared."

"Well, get over it. I give unprepared speeches all the time."

"That may be true for you. You're in sales. She sits in a cubicle designing firewalls and internet security systems. Why didn't you congratulate her without calling her up? And you also made her look bad in front of everyone when you said, 'Mary barely knew what she was doing when she arrived.'"

"But she didn't! She was brand new! Anyone can appreciate that! I was being funny!"

"No, you were being rude. *You* may have appreciated the message. Mary didn't. Never insult a perfectionist by pointing out her imperfections. She may have weaknesses—don't we all? But that doesn't mean she wants them made public. I'm a bit surprised you didn't read her a bit better. She's been working for you for almost five years!"

To be clueless in the workplace means that you unknowingly speak in a way that distances your listener. You disengage.

You alienate others, making it difficult for them to accept and respond to your ideas.

We fall into this trap when we miscalculate.

Wow! I thought she'd appreciate being brought up in front of the room!

I had no idea this would be boring for my team!

Well, how was I supposed to know he's computer illiterate? This is who I am. I'm not going to explain it to him. He can learn it on his own!

I don't know why people are so sensitive. I try to give helpful advice and they take it the wrong way.

Every day, in every office, people want to be themselves. The idea of customizing a message for someone else seems time-consuming and overwhelming. It's much easier to function within our own style than adapt to someone else's personality, even for a short time. Nevertheless, that's what we have to do in order to create rapport.

It seems obvious that Joel treated Mary the way he wanted to be treated, not the way she wanted to be treated. That little piece of humiliation, shame, and embarrassment cost Joel a lot of grief. Mary was deeply upset. She called in sick for the next two days. Other employees now live in fear that they may be put on the spot some day, and Joel earned a reputation for being a big fat jerk.

How could this have been avoided?

Joel could have approached Mary more indirectly, more cautiously because that's how she wants to be approached: "Mary, if giving a speech would make you uncomfortable, I'd understand, but we'd love you to say a few words. Would you do that?" Knowing Mary is not social (like he is) and acknowledging that fact might help him accept her answer. "I'm not comfortable giving a speech, and thank you for asking."

End of story.

Learning to adapt your approach to meet the needs of your audience is absolutely essential. Even Donald Trump, whose famous slogan, "You're fired," sums up his direct personality style, isn't always direct. He can lower his dominance and even raise his sociability level. Who would think a man with his high assertiveness and East Coast sophistication would put on denim overalls and sing the theme song to "Green Acres" on national television?

Anyone can adjust his or her style. Here are some strategies for doing just that:

The Basic Premise: Treat People the Way They Want to Be Treated.

Delivering messages that create rapport is the easiest way to retain employees, create appreciation, and instill high morale. According to Tony Alessandra, author of *Relationship Strategies*, you can do this by asking yourself two questions. The answers to these questions will help you know your listeners, and then customize your communication style to get what you want.

Is the person I'm speaking to direct or indirect? Open or closed?

Direct/Indirect

Direct people seek the core message, perhaps occasionally skipping over details. Direct people are often assertive. "Here's the bottom line. This is what I want you to do and here's why." Direct people tell instead of ask, and they tend to handle confrontation well, without shying way from it. "You're fired!" tells it like it is.

Indirect people feel less comfortable confronting others and, to their credit, they tend to make certain all their ducks are in the row before making a decision. "I don't want to fire

Phillip until we make sure we're following all the rules." They probe and research before drawing conclusions. "I want to ask a few questions before I make a decision."

Direct people, on the other hand, are more likely to make instant decisions, and this decisiveness is often their strength. However, the direct approach can wear thin and rub people the wrong way. This book, in some ways, is dedicated to those direct people who simply drop verbal bombs without thinking. Words plop out. They'll admit, "I can't believe I said that!" Direct people naturally, instinctively say what they have to say and seek forgiveness afterwards.

Indirect people may also face consequences from their behavior. They hold emotions in and then explode. Their patience and attention to detail can be huge assets, but they also tend to be indecisive. By waiting too long, they miss opportunities and frustrate people who have a more direct communication style.

Yet, both approaches—direct and indirect—are vital to any organization.

When you address top level managers who take great risks, assume responsibilities for the company, and reap rewards accordingly, you should speak their language. These are people who don't want their time to be wasted. They hate being hustled. They distrust language that tends to soften or "weaken" the message.

Now, shift the audience from upper management to middle management—customer service or front office—and you may need a more indirect approach that acknowledges and appreciates responsible feedback. Indirect people can be more sensitive. They want to be asked first, not told. Their feelings matter and they will react badly to rudeness, indifference, and aggressiveness.

"Please, won't you be my neighbor?" Mr. Rodger's famous slogan cordially invites children to create friendships and close relationships by probing and being kind to others.

The Mouth Trap

Imagine Donald Trump's direct approach as a children's show entitled *Be My Neighbor!* He would insist children learn networking and thinking strategies to hone their entrepreneurial skills. One episode might be called: "Don't Take No For an Answer."

Though many of us may lean in one direction most of the day, taking a direct or indirect approach toward problems and issues that arise, we undoubtedly move in and out of both styles.

You probably use the direct and indirect approaches all the time in your daily interactions.

> ➤ Direct: "Eloise, I need these papers by 4 p.m."
> ➤ Indirect: "Eloise, thanks so much for your contributions this morning at the meeting. I'd like these papers for the Cohen account by 4 p.m. today. Can you do that for me?"

A sensitive people-person might dub the first request as cold, even offensive. A no-nonsense, direct personality, however, who wants her messages bullet-pointed at a fast and furious pace, might find the second message patronizing. *Don't waste my time with all those extra words!*

Open/Closed

Do you enjoy parties where you can drift around the room, introducing yourself and making new friends? Would you turn to a complete stranger sitting next to you on the plane and start a conversation? Sometimes "open" people are accused of sharing "too much information," and the downside can be that you reveal things about your life you later wish you had never shared.

If the previous description doesn't fit, perhaps you're more self-contained. People can't easily read your emotions or thoughts. You share when it's time to share. You only talk about what's necessary and would never be accused of blabbing. You're focused and stay on target. The downside? Because you're hard to read, people may see you as aloof, distant, or disinterested.

Open people—sometimes called extroverts—gain energy by interacting with others, and they're often accused of "thinking with their mouths." Sentences roll off their tongues, sometimes too easily. Closed people, or introverts, get energy from being in their own brains and inside themselves. This makes them appear distant and aloof. They value private space. In *How to Spot a Liar*, Greg Hartley and Maryann Karinch point out that introverts with high energy will often be seen "rehearsing what they're going to say before they're going to say it, mumbling to themselves when alone."

Reading People

To determine someone's personality, find out how well the person deals with confrontation. Let's go back to Joel, our software salesperson/manager. Joel confronts issues directly, but he isn't a people person. He prides himself on thinking outside the box and often puts his foot in his mouth because he won't customize his message to his audience. Hence, Joel is direct and closed.

Remember Pierre, our imaginary prime minister of France? Is he open or closed? Direct or Indirect? Because Pierre avoided confrontation, we can assume he's indirect. He thrives on the love and attention of others, which tells us he's open. On the surface, Pierre is everyone's best friend and people enjoy being around him, but beneath that friendly exterior seethes a hidden agenda. Pierre holds onto "stuff" until he gets an opportunity to explode. That's rarely a good thing.

Can we change between open/closed and direct/indirect? For example, could Joel ever be expected to take Mary aside before the dinner and ask, "Do you mind if I call you up to the podium?" Can Joel learn to take a more indirect approach? Absolutely. Will it come easily to him? No. He'll need to learn and practice this approach, but it will keep him from sticking his foot in his mouth.

So Joel could either switch gears—become more sociable and empathetic for 30 minutes—or, if that isn't comfortable, he might delegate that task to someone else. In life, don't we do that at times? In every aspect of our businesses, we hire people who are better at certain tasks than we are. After all, we can't do everything!

Joel also could have "clued" into Mary's personality. She's indirect and closed. She speaks very little at work and spends most of her time in a cubicle working on the computer. Isn't that enough evidence to realize she may not want to give a speech in front of a roomful of strangers? She was also hired for her ability to design error-free security systems for the company's software: She pays attention to every single detail. What makes Joel think she would just spontaneously, without any preparation, stand up and give a speech? Having some knowledge of Mary's personality—her quadrant—would have saved Joel the grief of possibly losing one of his best employees.

The Four Quadrants

Based on the behavior and the two questions I raised earlier, most experts divide personalities into four quadrants. During an average work day we may cross boundaries and work in all four quadrants, but our comfort zone is usually embedded in just one of them.

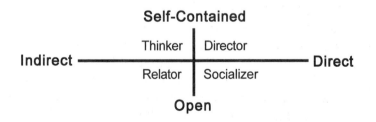

84

You can identify yourself and the personality of the person you're speaking to by asking two questions and placing yourself in a particular quadrant. Is the person direct or indirect? Open or closed?

Detail-Oriented Thinkers (Closed/Indirect)

If you are not a detail-oriented thinker, but you're married to one, think twice before washing the dishes. Every missed crumb will be discovered. Every Cheerio you leave behind on the counter will be accounted for. Now the thinkers' gift to you and me: They think it out! They value the facts. They're perfectionists. They make sure everything is done in an organized, detailed manner. Nothing is left out. The trap? They think too much. They work so hard at perfectionism that their projects may run late. They overanalyze, sometimes to the point of paralysis by analysis. Though they probably don't often say the wrong thing, the silence can be stifling. If they stop speaking, and you call them on it—"You haven't talked to me all day!"—they'll correct you. "It's only been seven hours and 15 minutes." When dealing with thinkers, leave plenty of time for the appointment and realize their greatest fear is making mistakes, leaving something out, or forgetting a comma. Their greatest contribution to humanity? *Dragnet.* They "pore" over every detail to uncover and unravel "just the facts."

Visionaries or Socializers (Open/Direct)

Thinkers have trouble with socializers who talk too much and tend to be disorganized. Socializers, though, have fun. They drive cars that are too short for their heads. Their backseat will hold two children, but they have five. They can't hear the music on the car radio because the motor on their sports car is so loud, but they look awesome with the convertible top down. They love to walk their dogs in neighborhoods and meet people. And they dress for the occasion. "How's it going?" is a favorite expression. Their cell phones are usually colorful and always on, especially in movie theatres and restaurants.

Approach socializers with energy and enthusiasm. If you tend to hide your emotions, they'll consider you boring. For a few seconds you might smile, show interest, use open posture, lean forward, and ask a few questions. Compliment socializers and never embarrass them in front of others. The worst thing you can do is to cut them off. If you let them speak without restrictions, they'll bury you with words. Their gift to mankind? Happy hour. They're animated, lively, entertaining, and fun.

Consensus-Driven Relaters (Open/Indirect)

Often called the "water cooler" people, these folks drive minivans, belong to clubs, enjoy picnics, and will join a bowling league even if they hate bowling. They love people. Their favorite expression? "Who else is going?"

On the upside, they are fair, loyal, and cooperative. The down side? They tend to be oversensitive, can't make decisions, and hold feelings inside instead of expressing them. Ever heard of passive-aggressive? Relaters are often guilty of saying, "No problem," when they truly do believe there is a problem. Tucked inside their bellies, the problem will eventually re-surface as a verbal tirade. Put the relater on your "fab five" phone list. Their greatest gift to you? They're great listeners. But do they make decisions? Well, listen to two relaters and find out:

"Where do you want to go lunch?"

"I don't know. Where do you want to go?"

"I don't know! Where do you want to go?"

"Wherever you want to go is fine with me."

"Arby's?"

"Doesn't excite me, but if that's what you want, I'll go."

When you interact with relaters, be expressive, casual, and informal. They read things into situations, so your communication should be sincere and up front. If you approach relaters for a project, tell them how much you appreciate having them on the team, and don't be afraid to include them as arbitrators when communication issues arise at work.

Directors (Closed/ Direct)

These folks run the show. They take responsibility seriously and work at a faster pace than the other personalities. They can't tolerate laziness and desire a straight-forward approach. "Stop wasting my time" is a favorite expression, so before you approach a director you should know the outcome you want, have an agenda, and streamline your message.

Can they be jerks? You bet. Are they competitive, challenging, demanding, and controlling? Often. Do they appreciate short descriptions of themselves? Yes. Oh, their greatest "contribution" to the planet? They run it.

Competing Styles

In the example mentioned earlier, Mary's analyzer/thinker personality may be a wide contrast to Joel's more direct, bottom-line director approach, but their traits are a tight fit for their jobs. Mary analyzes data and Joel gives sales pitches to clients.

These competing styles help make their business work. Can you imagine what life would be like if your company only hired people with one of these styles? That could be a disaster!

Years ago I taught a seminar made up of 25 directors—in other words, 25 Joels. During the day, two of them got into a fistfight and one had to be rushed to the hospital. We honestly needed other personality styles to mitigate the dominance in the room. They all wanted control!

The Mouth Trap

Perhaps you can remember the film *War of the Roses* with Kathleen Turner and Michael Douglas, two highly dominant people who fight for their rights and kill each other as they swing on chandeliers. Every relationship needs balance. That's why opposites attract.

Most companies prefer a combination of management styles. You may have a Hummer-driving boss who is autocratic (direct and closed), but is complemented by a Ferrari-driving vice president who encourages a positive image, fun, and community involvement (open and direct.)

President Sal (who drives the biggest Mercedes ever to leave Stuttgart) is a tough-minded director who depends on his vice president (his wife—a combination relater/socializer) to clean up any mistakes he makes. Her favorite phrase is, "What Sal means is...." And "Oh, he didn't mean anything by that."

When direct people say something wrong, indirect people move in to clear the slate and erase hard feelings. We often see this in families. One tough-minded parent makes a hasty decision—"You have to be home by 10 p.m."—and the other parent mops up the tears and attempts to create a consensus. "It's okay, honey. Be home at 11, but don't tell your father I talked to you."

Isn't there a better way?

Why can't tough-minded people become more consensus driven? And why can't those closed, analytical types see the big picture once in a while? Why can't we control or adjust our approach so we can get what we want without creating resistance? In other words, what would it take to get Mary to think outside her "thinker" quadrant and improvise a speech for ten minutes? Or, for that matter, could Joel appreciate the inherent genius of Mary's Web design and realize—*giving speeches is not her strength. I don't want to do anything to embarrass her.*

In the earlier chapters we looked at a variety of strategies that can help us prepare and think before we speak. We also examined ways to listen carefully even in times where we feel disinterested or bored. Equally important is this skill to determine quickly and effectively who we're speaking to before we ever open our mouths, customizing our message so we get exactly the outcome we're seeking. Here are tips for achieving that:

Adjusting Our Style

In his book, *The Entrepreneur Next Door*, Bill Wagner studied assessments of thousands of employees. Based on this research, he believes we have great difficulty maintaining uncommon behaviors for long periods, but we all have the ability to change our styles long enough to achieve specific outcomes. For example, you may not be particularly analytical or detail oriented, but you can apply that behavior for 15 minutes when you proofread a report or balance a checkbook. An analytical type, on the other hand, could raise her sociability for 10 minutes at an office party so she appears involved and team oriented instead of indifferent and aloof.

The four qualities within our personalities include dominance, compliance, patience, and sociability. Each quadrant discussed earlier contains different levels of these qualities. To be successful and meet the needs of our audience, we make adjustments.

Those of us with high levels of **dominance** seek control. "I want it this way." Highly dominant people (most often Directors or Socializers) run offices, manage people, and rule the world. As parents, we often lower our levels of dominance when we're asking our children's teachers to be more patient, more cooperative, more understanding; however, we might raise the dominance if dealing with sensitive issues in which no compromise can be made. "Joey has to miss class today because this is the only time the doctor can see him. Please reschedule his test."

People with low levels of dominance tend to be more passive. They would often avoid or shy away from confrontation and feel more comfortable in an environment in which people interact and get along. A less dominant approach with a teacher might sound like this: "I don't want to step on any shoes. I understand you have rigid standards, but is there anything you could do this time to allow Joey to take this test at another time?"

Sociability refers to our people skills. High levels are often seen in people who spend great deals of time dealing with customers, training employees, and speaking with the public. But if sociability is too high, a person goes off on tangents, tells unnecessary jokes, and talks on the phone too long. Sometimes higher levels cause distraction or irritation and zap productivity.

When we see lower levels of sociability, we often witness quieter, more introverted people. Those who read documents all day or pore over figures probably need a low level of sociability. On the other hand, if these people are forced to communicate in tough situations, they can sometimes be far too quiet, brooding, even complacent.

Compliance measures our ability to follow rules. With high levels, you do as you're told, and you have little difficulty sticking to the rulebook. One might expect, for example, an accountant or a construction worker or an engineer for NASA to have high levels of compliance because certain rules have to be followed. We want our taxes done right without an audit. If I have cabinets built in my garage that will hang over my car, I want every bolt correctly installed in the studs so it doesn't fall on my brand new hybrid. That installer probably needs a high level of compliance, making certain the job is done perfectly, adhering to every detail of the blue print.

With low levels of compliance, you break or adjust the rules. Such flexibility allows you to create unconventional ads, sell used cars, create new products, and re-invent the world. If you have a job that requires adherence to regulations (such as an accountant) and yet you have an instinctive lack of compliance, you might be a great asset to the firm for you might re-think and reinvent faster ways of getting things done. The downside of low compliance in an accounting firm might be somewhat obvious: these people are more prone to fudge the numbers, making the company vulnerable to a federal investigation or a law suit.

Relaxation/patience. Those with high levels of relaxation can do repeatable tasks and have an uncanny level of persistence. Mr. Rogers, for example, taught children the value of taking one's time. He'd remove his sweater at the beginning of each program and hang it carefully on a hanger. His voice, often soft and modulated, helped children relax. Raising our level of patience is especially important when we want to pay attention to details (that is, proofreading our e-mails).

Lower levels of patience suggest a drive to get things done. Fast paced and easily excited, the teams on *The Apprentice, The Great Race*, and other reality shows tend to move fast and multi-task to meet their goals. Most leaders, one would suspect, tend to move expeditiously toward their goals and perhaps that is why they're often described as "driven."

Because each of us tends to "live" with a familiar, innate behavior that we've been practicing all our lives, it may be difficult to make adjustments. For example, if you are accustomed to having very high levels of relaxation—you're an auditor—and you spend most of your time checking charts and tables, one might suspect you'd have difficulty taking over a task that involves fast, sometimes impetuous decision making.

Mary—the shy software security engineer—was drawn to a profession that relies little on interpersonal connections so giving a speech is quite foreign to her. Frankly, her dilemma is fairly typical of millions of business professionals across the country: Many people freeze in situations in which they are forced to be outspoken and sociable. One of the greatest fears among American business professionals? Getting up in front of a room and giving a speech. But can Mary do this for a small period of time? Absolutely. She joins Toastmasters. She takes a speech class. She practices using a tape recorder, and for five or 10 minutes, she can deliver impromptu speeches that are lively and animated. When she's done, she may feel exhausted and relieved, but it's a skill she can learn and take on for small periods of time.

So here's the trap: How do we move outside the "comfort zone" and become who we need to be at certain moments during the day? How do we raise and lower our levels of compliance, sociability, dominance, and patience so that we can adjust to certain situations and create the outcome we want?

At times this may seem very difficult. Highly dominant people who are forced to "just listen" or "not do anything" feel challenged in situations where they can't call the shots. It's extremely uncomfortable for them, just as those with low levels of dominance grow nervous and anxiety ridden when they are forced into situations where they have to call the shots and make decisions.

Can we make these adjustments more easily?"

Most experts believe that no matter how long we've practiced or maintained certain behaviors, most of us have the ability to switch gears and take on other behaviors for small periods of time. It may not be easy, for example, for a highly driven, energetic, high pressure salesperson to slow down and take careful measurements while designing a customer's closets, but for 11 minutes, that salesperson could—with the right mind set—raise her patience and compliance level and perform that skill. Very often we may hear people at work say, "That's not my job. I'm not good at that!" "This is just who I am. Don't expect to be someone I'm not." Well, that may be very true, but great communicators have the ability to dip in and out of different behaviors. Now it may be true that, at the end of the day, if you've been taking on a personality that goes against the grain of who you are, you'll be exhausted. And if the behavior you take on goes unappreciated or ignored, you'll easily revert back to who you really are. Nevertheless, the commitment we make to developing the skills—even those which are foreign and uncomfortable to the very essence of who we are—often make or break our ability to win an argument, make a deal, or earn a promotion.

Coaching Bryan

I recently coached Bryan, a seminar leader who received negative comments because of poor organization: He would switch topics without rhyme or reason and fail to understand and address specific concerns of his audience. One participant claimed, "Mr. Bryan boarded the Bryan train, never looking out the engineer's window to see if anything blocked the tracks." The participant went on with the extended metaphor to say, "He never stops at stations along the way, and he switches tracks randomly, reaching destinations where no one wants to go."

At the same time, Bryan was a thrilling speaker. For socializers, he was a fun, exciting storyteller who interacted and played games.

"Best time I've ever had in a seminar."

"I wasn't bored for one second."

You can't please everyone, but for Bryan to meet the needs of an entire audience (including "thinkers"), he needed to raise his level of compliance and organize his material carefully so it followed a format the thinkers would appreciate. In addition, he had to recognize, research, and acknowledge the requirements of his audience and address these points during the speech or through a question-and-answer at the end.

Finally, Bryan needed to increase his relaxation level and slow down. Not everyone could think as fast as Bryan. Instead of being Speed Racer, he should add a little Jimmy Carter.

After revising his agenda and re-tooling his seminar, Bryan told me that at the end of the day he'd never experienced such exhaustion in his life. "I'm telling you, Gary, to follow an outline and stick to it is the hardest thing I've ever done in my whole life."

Raising his levels of compliance and relaxation consumed a lot of energy because it didn't come naturally to him. At the same time, Bryan had to lower his social-ability and take that quality of openness—so natural to his personality—and stick it into his back pocket. At Happy Hour, he could retrieve it when he met with friends after work.

For 10 minutes, I can absolutely be more assertive. I can take 'em on.

Wow. I'm dealing with accountants here. I'd better pay attention to the details.

I know I have a big mouth. I'm going to lower my level of sociability so I don't say the wrong thing...

Imagine Patton

Imagine for a moment the great general and strategist George Patton was alive today. During his lifetime, Patton's high level of dominance placed him in hot water on many occasions. He slapped a couple of soldiers. He treated shell-shocked men in the infirmary as cowards. He littered his speeches with four-letter words and refused to watch what he said when he was being filmed for newsreels. Eventually his foot-in-mouth disorder alienated him from General Eisenhower and forced him out of certain key battles near the end of the war. But let's just pretend for a moment that he's alive today, running for president. Would these behaviors work in his favor? Would his low level of sociability win him votes? Certainly not. If he wants to appeal to the voters, he'll have to raise his sociability on TV and in rallies, lower his dominance when speaking to his staff, but raise it during debates when he'd be challenged by his opponents.

Could Patton pull it off? Probably not. His low level of sociability and high level of dominance would seep into his conversations and get him in trouble constantly.

Could he support another candidate and speak for that person with some panache, some warmth, for 15 minutes? A gentler, nice side of Patton? Absolutely.

Most of us have the ability to assume a behavior foreign to us. Almost anyone can slide in and out of a behavior that will help him handle a situation appropriately. Will it be easy to do? No, but raising and lowering these characteristics greatly assist us in getting the outcome we want, every time we have a conversation.

Action Steps

In order to engage almost anyone, say the right thing, and obtain the results we want, it's vital to understand the personality style of our listeners. Remember Tony Alessandra's The Platinum Rule: Treat others the way they want to be treated. We can determine personality several ways:

1. Ask ourselves two questions: "Is the person I'm speaking with direct or indirect? Is he or she open or closed?"

2. We can either probe and ask questions, or watch and listen. Direct people are usually more animated, use physical gestures, state ideas emphatically, and are less intimidated by confrontation. Indirect people ask questions (probe), and tend to be more cautious and hesitant.

3. Open people are easy to spot, because they're open! Open handshake, open smile. They aren't

afraid to share their souls. Closed people are more standoffish and if you want information, you may have to pull it out of them. They're harder to read. You can look at an open person and almost sense what they're thinking; not so with closed people, who shelter their emotions.

4. In order to more carefully understand the four quadrants, consider the elements that make up our personalities: dominance, compliance, relaxation, and sociability.

5. Remember, we may feel comfortable in one particular quadrant, but, in life, we're constantly shifting. Though experts believe most of us always go back to the quadrant we're born to inhabit, we each have the ability to take on other behaviors for short periods of time.

6. Adjusting our conversation to a particular personality is especially important at work, because when we want someone to do something—return a project, finish a letter, attend a meeting—we're usually more successful if we speak that persons' language and think as they do.

And now I have a question for you...

Case Study #1

Debbie was just promoted to manager. She walks through the office with a huge smile on her face. She's kind and sweet. People say, "Debbie is just a breath of fresh air. She never gets on your case. She's always saying, 'No problem. Don't worry about it.'"

Ned, one of her employees, starts coming in late several times a week. He tells Debbie his kids just started school and his wife has a new job. They're having problems getting organized. He assures her, "I'm trying the best I can."

Debbie tells him, "No problem."

But it is a problem. Ned controls production, and when he's late for work, his installers get a late start. Not only that, but those who work under Ned figure—"Our boss is late— why should we come on time?"

Debbie's boss coaches her: "You need to tell Ned he can't be late. It's affecting his team. The other guys in the shop resent him, and he's breaking company policy."

Debbie puts this off. Indirect and open, she fears giving direction. She also feels sorry for Ned. What should she do?

Case Study #2

Chris, a 21-year-old employee, takes a job that involves travel back and forth from New York to Los Angeles. He's a born salesperson: outgoing, energetic, and quite dominant. He often arrives late to the airport and on one occasion misses his flight and has to pay an additional fee for his next flight. (His work does not reimburse him.)

So months go by and Chris raises his level of compliance: he shows up hours early so he won't miss his flight. All goes well until one day, while waiting in the terminal for the airplane, he falls asleep and misses the flight. Again, he has to pay for a new ticket—but this time he argues with the airline supervisor and gets kicked out of the airport.

(He also loses his job.)

Be Chris's coach. You're his next employer. What behavior does he need to practice on a regular basis in order to keep a job and be successful?

Devil's Advocate: Well, I waited to the end this time, because I don't believe people behave predictably the way you describe them. I'm not in any one of those quadrants; I constantly shift from one to another. My Myer's-Brigg's brands me in the director/controller quadrant, yet I sometimes let people make decisions. I can balance my checkbook and think out the details. I did great in math and science in school. I actually love dancing, and when I'm at parties with my friends, I can be animated and lively. So I hate to be pigeonholed, and don't appreciate being told, "You're a Director—and that's the end of it."

Dr. Gary: First of all, if you were to choose one quadrant—one place where you feel most comfortable—would it be in the top two or the bottom two?

Devil's Advocate: Well, I don't know. I...

Dr. Gary: Don't give me that baloney. There isn't an indirect bone in your body. You like to take control, right? Even when you let others take over, you're thinking—what can I do to interrupt? Would you be happy working for someone else your entire life?

Devil's Advocate: Hell, no.

Dr. Gary: Do you like to argue?

Devil's Advocate: What do you think?

Dr. Gary: We know nothing about you except the issues you raise. You never once spoke of your family life, where you live, or what you do for a living. You're closed. And you rarely hold back, so you're direct. The fact that you feel you can assume other characteristics from other quadrants suggests your flexibility. Nothing wrong with that, but we got you pegged, man.

Chapter Five
The Joy of Scripting
Recipes for Conversing
in Even the Most Difficult Situations

> *The real art of conversation is not only to say the right thing at the right place but to leave unsaid the wrong thing at the tempting moment.*
>
> *—Dorothy Nevill*
>
> *Words are, of course, the most powerful drug used by mankind.*
>
> *—Rudyard Kipling*

This is how a boss from years back used to talk to me:

"Gary, I'm not a fan of bouillabaisse. I like to know what I'm eating. In bouillabaisse (or fish stew as it's sometimes called) chefs toss almost everything into the stewpot that swims in the ocean except license plates. You have to wear a bib to eat it. It takes forever to finish, and unlike most soups, this one takes endless chewing, spitting, and swallowing. It's just a mess.

"Connors wants to go for bouillabaisse tonight, and I don't have the time to sit there waiting for him to finish. I'd appreciate it if you talk to him; let him know we just have an hour. I promised my wife, whom I've barely seen all week, that I'll be home by 9 p.m., and bouillabaisse won't work for me. Chili's or Outback would work fine, if there's no line. So see what you can arrange, and get back to me, okay?"

Originally from New Orleans, my boss had a languorous style of speaking that might be charming on a lazy August afternoon, while sitting on the veranda drinking cold lemonade. On a Thursday at 5 p.m., however, when I desperately wanted to get home, he was the last person I wanted to hear.

Had I been in a position to "coach" him, I would have suggested he edit his stories at work into a tight, structured format so people wouldn't duck for cover every time he walked by. His sentences were like bear traps; once they grabbed hold of you, they wouldn't let go, sometimes for hours. A revision of Mr. Bear trap's monologue might go something like this:

"We're having dinner with Connors tonight, but I want to make sure I'm home by 9 p.m. to be with my wife. The restaurant he wants to go to serves a famous bouillabaisse, but it will take an entire evening to eat, and I don't have the time for that. Would you call him and ask if we could change the venue to Outback or Chiles or something like that so I can be home by nine?"

1. Want/Obstacle/Resolution

Storytelling may well be a lost art form, and few of us work in environments in which we can relax and enjoy long narratives. We hear these long stories occasionally at conventions and keynotes, but many of us sleep through them or desert the room if we anticipate them. On weekends, it's a treat to sit with friends and hear each other's stories, meandering in and out of the past like time travelers. In business, however, time is money, and if you're going to speak more than a few minutes, what you have to say had better be awfully powerful or extremely funny.

The "Want/Obstacle/Resolution "revision you saw previously, based on a concept from communication expert Tom Hencshel, relies on a simple shortcut that allows the speaker to present material quickly and effectively so the listener can logically follow the train of thought.

What do you want? My boss wanted a one-hour dinner so he could go home to his wife.

What's in the way? Connors wants bouillabaisse, which takes more than hour.

Resolution: Call Connors and let him know that time is limited, so let's do Chili's. Another time, we'll do bouillabaisse.

Under pressure, we often respond emotionally to situations that "hook" us physically and verbally. We react rather than respond. Not meeting a deadline? Losing a customer? Being late again? Trying to schedule a dinner at the last minute? These situations trigger emotional responses.With little time to write things down, we often feel challenged, and the words stream out of our mouths—sometimes randomly and erratically. How can we speak our minds without ultimately damaging morale or hurting relationships?

Take a few breaths and think of the three words:

Want, Obstacle, Resolution.

Wrong Way:

> *Sam:We need to finish this today or else we're in big trouble, so here it is. Figure it out.That's all I'm going to say. Just do it! Take everything else off your list and have it on my desk by six tonight.*
>
> *Gary: But, it's Friday and I ....*
>
> *Sam:What did I just talk about at the meeting? This is a commitment. Get it done. And I don't want to hear another word out of you.*

Here's a revision.

Right Way:

> *Sam: I want this project completed before the weekend so I can bring it with me to the conference and share it with Hilary. My plane leaves tonight at 8.*
>
> *I realize you're swamped, but I'm willing to work with you. Let's look and see what tasks we can take off your agenda so we can finish this before my flight leaves. Okay?*

In this case, notice the speaker relied on specific, non-punishing concrete images. The deadline's spelled out. We know why. The speaker acknowledges the difficulty and asks for help in solving it. And you won't have to clean up the mess of angry, hostile, volatile spewing afterwards. People's "water" will stay intact. Morale won't dissipate. All will be well in the universe.

The Joy of Scripting

Scripts place us on a smooth and familiar track. They take us across known territory and at a comfortable pace, freeing our brains for more novel work. But then again, when we're on rails, we travel along the prescribed route with such finesse and ease that it's almost impossible to make an unscheduled turn.
—Kerry Patterson

"What I find truly frustrating," a new supervisor told me recently, "is that when Billy speaks, everyone seems to like him. He can tell you go to hell and make you want to buy the ticket to get there. But when I speak tough, I get grief. I don't know if it's what I say or how I say it, but as soon as I open my mouth, I'm in big trouble. What can I do differently? Are there special ingredients I need to follow?"

In the previous chapters we talked about creating clear, concise, thoughts that will help us design the outcome we want. We also looked at ways to use core language—concrete, memorable messages—that can be easily heard and understood. In this chapter, I'll go a step further and show you how to frame your ideas by scripting them so you can deal with confrontational situations.

The good news about "scripting" is it gives you a formula to follow that prevents you from meandering and moving off the subject. The bad news is that it can pigeonhole your ideas and force you to follow a framework that could be limiting.

Just as there's more than one way to cook a bouillabaisse, there are many ways to design a script.

Here are three more:

2. Behavior/Correction/Attitude

Pamela Jett-Aal in her wonderful CD program, *Communicate With Confidence,* suggests that when you want to change someone's behavior—whether you're asking a person to clean his desk, lower his voice, or come to work on time—remind yourself to sequence the thoughts:

BCA

1. Describe the behavior clearly and concisely. (**B**ehavior)
2. Tell the person what you want corrected. (**C**orrection)
3. Ask for that person's commitment. (**A**ttitude)

It goes like this:

I see you came in 15 minutes late today. You were 20 minutes late yesterday. I'd like you here on time so we're not picking up the phones for you and dealing with customer issues with which we aren't familiar.

Can I get your commitment on this?

The purpose of scripting is to help us avoid falling into unscripted territory—that land of bad ideas, stupid suggestions, and mindless thought. When we have a person coming in late to work, it's so easy to say something that will rub him the wrong way and cause retaliation, revenge, and hard feelings. Unscripted territory may cause us to say things like:

"Frank, you're **always** late."

"Frank, you're **never** on time."

"Frank, do you know what time you came in this morning?"

My favorite response: Raise your wrist so that the person sees your watch, take the index finger from your other hand and jab the faceplate of the watch, several times, as though performing Morse code.

Of course, there's always the schizophrenic compliment: "Oh yeah, thanks for coming in today. Is it lunch time yet?"

As with the **Want/Obstacle/Resolution**, this simple formula will point you in the right direction and adapts to a variety of situations, not just manager-to-employee.

"Jan, I noticed you were 20 minutes late this morning.

"I'm way behind with my own work because I answered half a dozen phone calls for you, and several of them were urgent.

"It would help a lot if you'd make an effort to be here at 8 a.m., and I'll do the same for you.

"Okay?"

The advantage of being specific is that no one can argue with the facts. If you said "You were late," the other party could deny it. The more concrete we are, the less likely we'll have an argument that creates defensiveness. Twenty minutes is real. Answering customer phone calls—six of them—is concrete.

The **correction** *only* works if you have a compelling reason behind it. If Jan doesn't care, she probably won't change her behavior. If she doesn't like you, she may come in late on purpose just to irritate you. So it's important to make certain Jan agrees with your thought: that coming in late does indeed create a burden for others. If she doesn't agree to that, you won't get her to buy in.

Also, the listener (Jan) wants to know what's in it for you, the speaker. Will you gain more than she will? In her book, *Story Factor,* Annette Simmons agrees that knowing "what's in it for the listener" is important. The listener needs to identify the speaker's motives. "No matter what people say about 'what's in it for you,' potential self-interest, reasons why, or logical justifications, we filter every word through a believability index based on our judgments about who they are and why they are here.... When you focus all your communication on showing your listener what he might gain, you come across as hiding your gain."

To create clarity and make certain the BCA is effective, you need to identify the perspectives of both the listener and the speaker. You can do that by asking questions to uncover the problem. It might go like this:

>**Jan**: *Sally, you were 20 minutes late again. What's going on?*
>
>**Sally**: *What?*
>
>**Jan**: *We discussed this yesterday. I'm depending on you. Tell me what's happening. Mrs. Angelas is your client. She was emphatic about speaking to someone first thing, and I hope I handled her correctly, but I'm frustrated. I know nothing about her case.*
>
>**Sally**: *I'm doing the best I can. I couldn't get the kids out on time. They're driving me crazy.*

Note: Sally does not yet recognize the thought. She's only seeing her perspective: "I'm doing the best I can."

>**Jan**: *I thought we made a commitment a few days ago to be in the office by 8 a.m. so we're not handling each other's clients. Was I wrong?*
>
>**Sally**: *No, it's just that I'm not used to the new school schedule and...*

(Don't interrupt her. I know it's painful, but here she might be getting to the heart of the problem)

Sally: *I know I said I'd be here on time, but I don't know what the big deal is. You come in late sometimes. I cover for you. Why can't you cover for me?*

Now we have a better idea what the problem is: Sally thinks it's okay to come in late because of some mythical agreement. If Jan wants to get Sally's buy-in and understanding, she has to encourage Sally to understand the thought: It is not okay to come in late. No agreement exists on that.

Jan: *Sally, that was not our agreement. The problem is, you tell your customers you'll be in at 8 a.m., right?*

Sally: *I don't know.*

Jan: *Come on.*

Sally: *I do, yes.*

Jan: *And when you're not here at 8 when they call, how do you think they feel?*

Sally: *I don't know.*

Jan: *Have you lost clients when you weren't here to take their phone calls?*

Sally: *(Silence)*

Note: Taking responsibility for our actions is one of the hardest, most painful acts we can experience. It's the moment of realization: I screwed up. Here's the reason behind it. If I continue doing this, I'll dig a deeper hole for myself.

Jan: *Why am I asking you to show up exactly on time?*

Sally: *Customers don't want to talk to a stranger. They want to talk to their rep. You can't do as good a job as I do with my clients.*

Jan: *You got it, girl! Let's add one more reason. They want to know you're reliable, right? And so do I!*

*Can I count on you to be here at 8 a.m. from now on,
so we don't have to discuss this again? Or, do we
need to change your hours?*

In the previous scenario, we were digging for gold—and ultimately we hit the payload: Sally thinks being late is no big deal because she believes Jan will deal with her customer issues.

Once you know the problem, you can address it.

Nothing will change unless you discover what's getting in the way. Sally might have considered the system unfair. She might think that 8:20 is like 8 a.m., because everyone else comes in late. In the back of Sally's mind, she might even harbor a memory of being late a year ago and no one made a big deal out of it, so why should they care now?

In this next example, based on a real incident, notice how the HR manager uses the BCA script on a supervisor to make him better understand the painful mistake he made.

Case Study: The Temp's Coke

In a plant where automobile transmissions are assembled, the rule is no personal items can be placed near the assembly line.

A temporary worker (Temp) put his almost-finished Coke (a couple of drops left) in front of him. Mark, the supervisor, picked it up and threw it in the trash.

Here's the dialogue that ensued. (I underlined the Temp's core message so you can see it. Notice how Mark ignores it.)

Temp: *I wasn't finished with that Coke, but you just grabbed it and threw it away.*

Mark: *Well, we have a rule here that you can't have personal items near the line.*

Temp: *I understand that, but I don't appreciate you reaching over me and grabbing something of mine.*

That was like a violation of my personal space. Next time, ask first.

Mark: *What do you think this is, a school for manners? I don't have to ask. I'm the supervisor here. You're a temp, and you should know the rules. We put you through orientation.*

Temp: *Look, I don't need to take your shit. All I'm asking is that you not reach over and put your fist in my face. Okay?*

Mark: *I'll put my fist in your face if I want to. Just follow the rules, or you're out of here.*

A fight ensues, and the manager breaks it up.

Angry and frustrated, the Temp walks off the line, muttering, "I don't need someone speaking to me like this." He goes directly to Mark's boss. A discussion follows between the three of them, and Mark apologizes for his language and promises to buy the Temp another Coke, but the Temp is still not satisfied.

Temp: *That's not the issue. I don't need another Coke. I'm upset that you grabbed it on the line and put your fingers in my face.*

Mark: *Man, what do you want from me? I promised I'd buy you another frickin' Coke! Stop your whining and take what I have to offer and get the hell out of here.*

So what's the real problem here? I underlined the core message *three times*, and Mark doesn't hear it. What is the Temp angry about and what does Mark *think* the temp is angry about? Uncovering the thought behind an issue is the first step to solving any problem. If Mark had done that, the Temp would probably have been satisfied and Mark wouldn't be facing performance evaluation problems or be a hostage in one of my workshops.

HR Manager: Mark, I see two issues here. Issue one: The Temp brought a bottle of pop on the line, which is a violation. I'll agree to that.

Mark: Thank you.

HR: Issue two: Did you handle it right?

Mark: I offered him another Coke!

HR: Did you handle it right?

Mark: No.

HR: What did you do?

Mark: I grabbed the soda.

HR: You grabbed it from him without asking, and that made him feel...

Mark: Oh, for God's sake.

HR: Uncomfortable and unsafe. Do you understand that?

Mark: I told him I'd buy him another Coke. What more did he want? He screws with me, and he's not going to get anywhere.

HR: You reached over and grabbed his Coke, which violated his personal space. What are we asking you to do? If you can't answer this, then we have a problem.

Note: The behavior has been defined clearly. Does Mark get it? Here's his self-correction.

Mark: (Correction): You want me not to reach over and violate personal space. Okay, but I offered to buy him another Coke.

HR: Did that solve the problem?

Mark: No.

HR: So what would have solved this particular problem?

Mark: I'm not supposed to reach over and do what I did. I'm violating his personal space. Golly Miss Molly. I'm not listening, am I? I just get so mad! I get so frickin' mad that I just want to burst. I don't think I could handle this any other way. This is just who I am.

HR: Walk away. Ask yourself, "What am I thinking?" You get paid to listen, Mark. That's why I made you supervisor. If you can't listen well, I'll either have to teach you or fire you. What's it going to be?

Mark: Buying him a Coke wouldn't solve this problem?

HR: What do you think?

Mark: I should apologize for reaching over and getting in his face.

HR: That's it.

The only way we "influence" behavior is for the person to truly buy into the thought. If Mark still believes the Temp's thought was foolish, the HR manager can try one more tactic:

Here's the BCA:

*HR: Mark, you say it like he's crazy, but if I did this to you (grabs Mark's pen from his shirt pocket) how does that make you feel? (**behavior**)*

Mark: Doesn't bother me a bit.

*HR: But it bothered him, and you're not listening to what bothers him or other people. That's truly what I'm asking for. Listen for the problem. Listen to the needs of others. (**Correction**) And then respond. Can you work on that for me? (**Attitude**)*

> **Devil's Advocate**: *This stuff is way too complicated. You're saying that before I use your Behavior/Correction/Attitude (BCA), I have to find out what the problem is first?*
>
> **Dr. Gary:** *Yes.*
>
> **Devil's Advocate**. *If you're telling me I have to unearth someone's thoughts, like some cosmic psychologist, you're off your rocker. I thought you were going to offer me fast scripts, not some long dialogue that take hours to finish.*
>
> **Dr. Gary:** *This technique doesn't take hours. In fact, that conversation took only a few minutes. You can't solve a problem unless you get the other person to take responsibility for the problem. That's my take on it.*

The quick, easy BCA happens once Mark understands and appreciates the issue. If the HR manager rushed into a solution without finding the thought behind it, Mark would not change his behavior. He might be cooperative for a couple of weeks, but unless he buys into the solution, he'll eventually revert back to his old behavior.

Of course, HR managers have an advantage because they can back up the BCA with a job description or a company policy. These policies may provide details regarding what employees can and cannot do in terms of touching, grabbing, and intervening in the personal space of others.

If you're delivering this message to a friend, family member, or fellow employee, you can't back up your words with a manual, but you can use personal experience and empathy. This next device will help you with that.

3. Feel/Felt/Found

This is an empathy device that works in situations where feelings matter.

I know how you feel. I have felt that way too. And I have found.

Mark feels frustrated over his inability to communicate well with the people who work under him, and the HR Manager feels Mark's pain. The **feel/felt/found** routine, though a bit warm and fuzzy, helps Mark understand he's not alone.

Right Way: "Mark, I know how you feel. Many times I have felt like just grabbing someone's personal item off the line. I have found, though, that everyone reacts differently in a work environment, and it's probably better to ask first. Do you think you can do that in the future?"

Wrong Way: A landlord, tired of elderly tenants calling him in the middle of the night to fix their toilets, yells at them, and says, "Will you stop calling me in the middle of the night? I'm not going to do anything until morning anyway! Jesus Christ!"

Better Way: Mrs. Cohen, I know how you feel. When I was a tenant I felt like calling my landlord in the middle of the night, but I found if I waited until morning, the landlord was a lot more receptive. Can you do that for me?

Warning: This method only works when feelings are important, and it doesn't work if you're insincere.

Wrong Way:

Jack: *Hattie, I understand your mother passed away and I'm so sorry. Hey, I know how you feel.*

Hattie: *Jack, did you lose your mother?*

Jack: *No.*

Hattie: *Then you really have no idea how I feel, do you?*

If you're sincerely empathetic, and you understand from past experience what this person is going through, this device works. Otherwise, skip it.

4. Feeling/Behavior/ Correction/Attitude

Here's the scenario: You take a day off to attend a work-related seminar, and while you're gone, people at work backstab and gossip about you. Rumor has it you go to a lot of seminars so you can get out of the office and prepare yourself for other work, maybe a different job.

The following statement is your first reaction. It does follow the formula—Feeling + BCA—but notice how *all* the information becomes overwhelming and makes it difficult for the listener to follow your train of thought. Like a thick soup, it contains far too many ingredients to consume in a short period of time.

"I'm concerned. I heard through the grapevine that people think I'm out of the office a lot and that I'm looking for another job. That isn't true, and I'd appreciate it if you do hear rumors, or if gossip is spreading, just come directly to me. I have a lot of reasons to go to these seminars, and much of it has to do with improving communication around here. I can call you during the day. I can arrange for times to answer any questions, but I don't want people gossiping at work and not addressing the issues directly. Understand?"

Ah, what?

Here's a revision—an entire conversation, including the search for the thought behind the office gossip:

> *Gary: John, I want to clarify a rumor I've been hearing. I understand you feel I go to too many seminars, and I'm not in the office enough. Is that true?*

The Mouth Trap

(Just as in our earlier examples, you can't change a behavior, unless the person recognizes it.)

Fred: That's not true, Gary. I never said anything like that. Where did you hear that?

Gary: You didn't share with others the thought that maybe I'm not here when you need me?

Fred: Well, I did have a problem last week. I needed to get hold of you, and you weren't here.

Gary: Where was I?

Fred: You were at a workshop.

Gary: And how did you feel about that?

Fred: I guess I was frustrated.

Gary: So you sometimes do have a problem with me not being here?

*Fred: Only in the sense that.... (**Bingo! Now we're getting somewhere**) it makes me jumpy. You seem to go to a lot of workshops. We're kind of thinking you're out there looking to leave.*

Gary: Leave here?

Fred: It just doesn't feel like your heart is in this job. You're always gone.

It isn't always easy to get the truth, but once it's out we can see it—it's tangible and recognizable. Just as it took some time to get Mark to realize his problem wasn't the Coke but the violation of personal space—here we have to make certain Gary recognizes what people are actually thinking. He has uncovered two issues: (1) He isn't available here when people need him, and (2) they think he has one foot out the door.

So Gary could make the following correction:

Gary: Look, if you'll call me right away next time, I'll get back to you within 30 minutes. Even in workshops, I check my voice mail via texting. Will that work for you?

(Wait for an answer.) And should you be
about my performance in the future, I wa
come directly to me and not to someone else.
that can be uncomfortable, but I'd much rather
from you than from the grapevine. Can you do

Now there's still the other issue—is Gary thinking of leaving the company? Handle each issue separately so you can be sure the other party hears you.

Gary: As far as looking for other jobs, it never crossed
my mind until I heard the gossip. I love this job, but I
don't like gossip. If people are just straight with me, I
may stay here for years. Understood?

Too much information confuses the listener, and no resolution takes place. Now this isn't to say we can't be firm and use consequences, but let us state the consequences in a context that will do the following:

> ➢ Avoid misunderstanding.
> ➢ Create an atmosphere for discussion rather than confrontation.
> ➢ Create a change in behavior without costly law suits or loss of jobs.

Action Steps

1. Write your script, but then toss it. Know it by heart.
2. Avoid "you" words and baggage words, such as: "always," "never," "should," and "can't." Even the words "need" and "should" create defensiveness.
3. Use "I" statements instead of "you" statements. "I felt embarrassed" instead of "you embarrassed me."

4. Include a non-baggage word or feeling if you feel it's necessary. These words are a great way to frame the conversation.

5. Stick to one topic at a time. Try and separate issues. Don't include several scripts in one conversation. Just get the buy-in after each script.

6. Bounce ideas off other people before you go into the office to deliver your script.

7. Know to whom you're speaking and customize the script for that audience.

8. Stand outside the mouth trap. Think as though you're in the listener's shoes.

9. What's the thought behind the behavior? Make the listener recognize the thought.

10. When delivering the script, check the other person's body language. Is she listening? Does she care? Do you need to stop and get buy-in?

And now I have a question for you...

Imagine you have an argument with a fellow employee regarding a lost "deposit check." You believe you've resolved the issue (you accidentally left it in the lunchroom), but at the next meeting your boss brings it up in front of the entire team and accuses you of mishandling money. You ask for a meeting with your fellow employee and the boss. What will you say?

Devil's Advocate: *If this were the best of all possible words and we could speak to people rationally like you describe here, these scripts might work. But I have the boss from hell. She's stubborn, aggressive, always right, and extremely successful. Though she's hardly a tyrant, she's a tough cookie, and I don't think this script format would work with her. She'd probably stop me mid-way through and say, "Cut the crap. You blew it! I'm angry." Do it again and you're out of here." How do you handle that?*

Dr. Gary: *The boss from hell is in the next chapter. Keep reading.*

Chapter Six

What Happens if I'm Speaking to a Big, Fat Jerk?

Navigating Around Difficult Bosses

> *Taking the high road isn't about smoothing things over or being too nice. It's about communicating effectively in a way that enables the listener to hear you and consider your ideas.*
>
> —Katherine Crowley/Kathi Elster,
> *Working With You is Killing Me*
>
> *All idiots might be created equal, but there is a wide disparity in how they are endowed by their Creator.*
> —John Hoover, *How to Work for an Idiot*

Seen the Boss From Hell Lately?

Some of the world's worst bosses come from the cinematic imagination of movie makers. Remember Franklin Hart Jr. from *9 to 5* whose misogynistic treatment of secretaries caused them to kidnap him and hold him hostage? Sigourney Weaver's portrayal of Katherine Parker from *Working Girl* is one of the most rude and arrogant bosses in film history. But let's not forget Meryl Streep in *The Devil Wears Prada* and the obnoxious boss in *Office Space*.

My personal favorite is Nurse Ratched from *One Flew Over the Cuckoo's Nest*. Ratched was a tyrannical, big-bosomed battle axe from hell in Ken Keasy's novel, but in the film, Louise

The Mouth Trap

Fletcher accentuates her vulnerability and humanity, making her even scarier than in the novel. No wonder Ratched made the top five of the 50 worst villains in film history. I bring this up for two reasons.

1. Thank your lucky stars you don't work for a fictional boss.
2. If you do work for an idiot boss, kidnapping, takeover coups, flame throwing, and infusing a virus into the company computer system may reward movie heroes, but in real life such crimes land people in jail.

It is unfortunate that in some businesses, life does imitate art, and according to Sutton in his book, *The No Asshole Rule*, occasions of incivility, bullying, and abusiveness directed by superiors to their subordinates run rampant. Recent data suggests, however, that businesses would be foolish to let such behavior continue without a check and balance system. Employees with abusive superiors quit their jobs, suffer depression, anxiety, burnout, health problems, feelings of worthlessness, chronic fatigue, irritability, and anger—all of which costs companies billions in liability laws suits, health care, and loss of productivity.

If I were to ask a group—what do you dislike most about your boss?—the answers are fairly standard. It isn't that bosses are 100-percent jerks—it's that they have jerk-like behavior.

➤ They micromanage.
➤ They lose their temper.
➤ They backstab.
➤ They favor one person over another.
➤ They don't communicate.
➤ They over communicate
➤ They hover.

> They give little or no feedback and then yell when you don't do it right.

> They never show appreciation for anything you do.

Seldom, by the way, do I ever hear someone say, "My boss compliments far too much. I can't stand it!" If any one characteristic seems typical of idiot bosses across the country, it is their lack of recognition, appreciation, and respect for all the hard work employees do.

So if you can't walk away from the problem or quit the job, what can you do to deal with bossy behaviors that drive people crazy? Here are a few techniques to consider.

Learn Their Stories

The Devil Wears Prada created a stir in the media because Anna Wintour, a real editor at *Vogue*, was widely believed to have been the inspiration for the story. Miranda Priestly—the devil in the title—ran a tight ship. Heartless, uncompassionate, defiant, and arrogant, her rigidity and cold demeanor eventually inspired the movie's heroine to leave the job and take what we might refer to as a "higher path." However, thanks to Merle Streep's excellent performance, critics commented that the real hero of that movie wasn't the nice narrator/assistant but the devil herself. Of all the people who worked at this fictional magazine, Miranda (Streep's character) cared the most and worked the hardest. No matter who plotted against her, she stayed in control. A mean spirited, bitchy ice queen, Miranda was a leader with ultimate survival skills.

If we worked with a boss like Miranda, the question might be: How did she make it? Why is her company such a huge success? What's her story, and what can I learn from her before I say something I might regret?

121

We may be decades passed the Age of Greed (remember *Wall Street* and the 1980s?), but we still see best-selling books that focus on leadership tips from Machiavelli, Attila the Hun, Hannibal, Patton, and other warriors. Even the books promoting good communication often focus on confrontation: *Difficult Conversations, Fierce Conversations,* and *Confrontational Conversations* are all titles of great books I've quoted here and used as references.

So, ask yourself: What about my tough, hard-to-deal-with boss am I not seeing? What can I learn from this person? Take the emotion out and focus on strategy.

When Martha Stewart hosted her own version of *The Apprentice*, a contestant, hoping his sincerity might win her over, admitted his faults and stated he should be fired—acknowledging his weaknesses on national television. Not surprisingly, Stewart—without a moment's hesitation—fired him on the spot.

He apparently forgot the Martha Stewart story: Never concede weaknesses. Always move forward, no matter what, because resiliency leads to success. If he knew what Martha went through—a humiliating trial followed by jail time and house arrest—one would think this young man could anticipate her expectations: Take the bad with the good and don't give up.

The Case of the X Generation Sales Rep

Five years out of graduate school, Jordan took a job with an insurance company in downtown Los Angeles, located 45 miles from his suburban home in Newbury Park. His commuting time was 90 minutes each way. Every morning he left at 6 so he could be at his desk by 8, but at least two nights a week he stayed at work until 11 p.m. to attend board meetings. His schedule was a nightmare. When he mentioned his problems to Gretchen, the vice president who hired him, she gave him a look. "I don't see what this has to do with anything," she finally said one morning. "You knew what you were getting into when we hired you. If I thought geographical distance would get in the way of your performance, I would have hired somebody else."

After being up all night with a sick 2-year-old, he came into work a half hour late and missed an important meeting. The boss didn't say a word, but Jordan suspected he should address the issue with her. He told her his baby was teething, and the baby simply didn't stop crying all night long. Though he set the alarm clock, he slept right through it.

Seeing little response on her face, he finally added: "I'm sure if you had kids, you'd understand how difficult it is."

Gretchen remained stone-faced through his explanation and walked out.

Jordan felt as if he'd stuffed several feet into his mouth.

Was he in trouble?

When he shared this incident with Lonnie, one of his racquetball buddies, Lonnie commented, "What a heartless bitch. She probably has no clue what we dads have to go through."

Gretchen's indifference continued. When she stopped inviting Jordan to important meetings and ignored his request to meet again, Jordan knew something was deadly wrong. Now he felt angry because she didn't even give him a chance to apologize.

He cornered Gretchen's assistant.

"You know I said something I shouldn't have a few weeks ago, and I'm trying to arrange a one-on-one with Gretchen. Any suggestions?" he asked.

"No," she snapped.

"Why not? I just want to meet with her."

"A little late for that now, don't you think?"

"Do I have to get on my knees and beg for mercy, for God's sakes?"

"May I make a suggestion? Jordan? You basically insinuated that Gretchen knows nothing about what you're going through because she's unmarried and doesn't have children. She finds that very insulting. You played the child card. She thought you were smarter than that. I'm afraid she no longer trusts you and refuses to work with you. Sorry. You're out on the fringe, boy. Better register on monster.com."

Jordan stammered, "I don't understand. I was just—I was just saying she may not see my side of..."

"First of all, her personal life is none of your business. She puts in 80 hours a week here. She helped create this company from scratch and turned it into a $25-million business. I've seen her work with no sleep at all. She runs marathons on no sleep, *and* she fought breast cancer. She's a very smart woman. You're a whining idiot. Next time, do your research and watch what you say before you open your mouth."

Jordan stumbled back to his office, speechless.

Now what?

I can't work with these women. They're nuts. They're lunatics!

A cappuccino later.

Maybe she's right. I should not have missed that meeting.

If she can't depend on me, then how am I going to prove myself as a sales rep and move up the ladder? I mean, would a young Donald Trump come in late to a board meeting and blame it on his kid? Probably not. But how was I to know that would bother her so much? Am I responsible for knowing all this before I open my mouth?

He asked the question to the wall, and the wall answered back. Well, he imagined the wall spoke, but it was a voice inside his head.

You blurted out an insult. If you knew your boss's story ahead of time, you would have chosen a different path. You could have just apologized for missing the meeting, and asked for some help. Instead of playing the child card, you could have said, let me think, I was afraid to drive on four hour's sleep. I apologize.

How do you avoid this mouth trap?

Knowing your boss's story will allow you to decide what goes into your conversation and what stays out. Making that decision—choosing your facts and sentences carefully—can make all the difference in the world, especially if you at least acknowledge your boss's point of view.

"If I only had known...." is an interesting phrase. Perhaps a better approach is, "I'm going to find out all that there is to know before I say anything." That may be the smarter road on which to travel.

Embrace the Resistance

Not every boss's argument is worth embracing. Depending on one's priorities, missing a meeting may be the right choice for us, but many times the demands are unreasonable and we opt to disagree.

"Well I'm just not going to show up at any of the meetings."

"If she's going to treat me this way, then fine. I'll move my allegiance somewhere else."

"You know what? Let her fire me. I had a very legitimate reason for coming in late. I haven't been here very long. I'll get unemployment and look for a job where I feel appreciated."

All these options, though, avoid responsibility.

Embracing resistance is a form of creative thinking. *What does my boss have in mind and how can I embrace it so that she knows I'm on her team, capable of acknowledging her ideas. I may not agree with her position, but I want to let her know that at least I'm listening and hearing her point of view.*

125

The Mouth Trap

In other words, had Jordan done his homework (learned her story), he would have known that Gretchen scraped and clawed her way to the top, doing whatever was necessary to reach success. Hence, a crying baby at home and a 45-mile commute are not her issues. They're his. Deal with them.

Instead of angrily "resisting" a boss's hard-headed, tough stand, he could have simply said, "You're right. It won't happen again."

End of story.

Devil's Advocate: Why doesn't he kiss her ass? I mean, the woman's a maniac! What are our priorities? Sometimes family comes first, and if she doesn't understand that, let the bitch know exactly how you feel.

Dr. Gary: First of all, my friend, be respectful. You're missing the whole point. Gretchen has her priorities. Jordan has his. According to the Oxford English Dictionary of Idioms, "Kiss ass" usually means—"to try too hard to please someone and to agree with everything they say, in a way which other people find unpleasant." Embracing resistance is different; it is a form of acknowledgement. Why does my boss want me to do this, and what's in it for me to do it?

We can embrace resistance without necessarily agreeing with the other person's position:

"Gretchen, I hear what you're saying. We should be at meetings on time. But I'm 26 years old, I have a baby, and I'm struggling with my priorities. Can we at least discuss it since I know this situation will pop up more than once?"

If you respect your boss's position, perhaps your boss will respect yours.

Discover what it is you're resisting and understand the other person's point of view. There is no surer way to shut down a conversation than to come into it with an entrenched position. Entering with an open mind may not necessarily embrace the situation, but you can certainly see all the facts and decide what parts you can embrace and what parts don't work for you. A good way to do this is to have what Douglas Stone, Bruce Patton, and Sheila Heen call the **three conversations**.

The Three Conversations

In their book *Difficult Conversations*, the authors describe three types of conversation:

1. The what happened conversation.
2. The feelings conversation.
3. The identity conversation.

In the Gretchen case study, Jordan and his boss only had one conversation: **What happened?** He was up all night with a crying baby. Gretchen, the boss, is thinking: Yes, and what does this have to do with the fact you missed a once-a-month meeting where your input was needed? You made me look bad.

Jordan took the conversation a step further and assumed she had no **feelings** for his plight (How could she? She doesn't have kids), and he bashed her **identity** as a woman. That one sentence "If you had kids, you'd understand" challenged her role as a single working woman.

Repair work is in order.

In asking for forgiveness, Jordan must recognize that Gretchen's assistant made it clear that it was too late to mend the situation, but if he wants to stay working as a sales rep, he has to say something to his boss.

> **Jordan:** *Look, I really blew it. I said something that I deeply regret.*

Gretchen: And what was that? I forget.

Jordan: I made a sexist comment that day in your office. I said, "If you had kids you'd understand." (What Happened?)

Gretchen: You know it's water under the bridge. I was mainly bothered that you were 45 minutes late to a board meeting. (What Happened?)

Jordan: It was only a half hour.

Gretchen: I looked at my watch at 7:45. You hadn't come in yet.

Jordan: I'm sorry.

Gretchen: Now as far as that comment you made. I know you're upset about that. Felicia told me. (Now we're moving on to feelings.) Don't worry about it. I know you didn't know what you were saying, but when the diversity training starts, take a front row seat.

Jordan: Thank you. So we're cool?

Gretchen: No.

Let's just stop here a moment. Though they both wisely focus on what happened (he quotes the inflammatory words), and they do discuss feelings (he's remorseful). Jordan also wisely asks about her feelings. "So we're cool?" Apparently, however, something else is going on in Gretchen's mind, and if you don't uncover all the issues, they'll remain hidden and haunt Jordan later on. Let's see what Gretchen wants:

Gretchen: To be honest with you, I feel I made a mistake hiring you. I should have known that the commute would get in the way. That's #1. And perhaps I overestimated your skills. You're right out of college. I need someone with more experience.

Jordan: So what does that mean?

Gretchen: The way you handled the situation, even the way you went to my assistant, instead of directly to me, that's not what I am looking for.

Jordan: I tried to see you on a number of occasions...

Gretchen: Let me finish. I'm not firing you. I think you need some years on you before I put you on a management pathway. Though I said at your interview I'd let you attend management meetings, I've changed my mind. You'll stay in sales, and when you prove yourself, I'll consider moving you into a management track. Are you okay with that?

When we speak up, as in this example, we often realize that what we think happened may be very different from our boss's perspective. In Jordan's case, he felt punished for what he said and if he wanted to stay at that company, he'd have to prove himself. From Gretchen's perspective, she acknowledges she made a mistake in overestimating several factors—his commute and his ability to communicate. Despite these barriers—which Jordan now sees quite clearly—his boss allows him to stay on board. It's up to him now to decide what he wants to do.

1. Either he deals with the commute and shows up on time, or he moves his family closer to work.

2. He watches the way he speaks and learns good communication skills.

3. He has to be willing to wait and prove himself before he can enroll in the company's management program.

Notice that by discussing their feelings and the impact it would have on both their identities in the company, Gretchen and Jordan have at least resolved a problem that had been festering for some time.

The Case of the Micromanaging, Hovering, Idiot Boss

Here's a situation that takes a slightly different approach. In this case, the employee may acknowledge her boss's perspective,

129

but she doesn't agree with it. Let's see what she does to fix the situation:

Sandy, a secretary, complained that her boss, Boris, often waited until 4 p.m. to give her important projects to do, making it difficult for her to leave work at 4:30. At first, she embraced the whole situation. After all, she had a good job. It was close to home. She also liked the people who worked with her.

After a few months, though, of working until 5 or 6 p.m., almost every day, she complained. "What are you worried about?" the boss would often tell her. "I stay until 7 or 8 p.m. sometimes! I'll make it up to you. I pay you overtime. You'll be just fine." She soon realized, though, that it wasn't the overtime she resented; it was his dismissive attitude. Implicit in his voice was this message: *You should have no problem with this. Be happy you have a job. Times are tough.*

Sandy's key to remedying the situation was non-confrontational. She figured out that the reason she had to stay late was because Boris didn't structure his time carefully. He'd saunter in past 2 or 3 p.m., open the mail, and then put on Sandy's desk—sometime around 4 p.m.—contracts for invoicing.

"Boris, I understand how important it is to finish these invoices and billings. I want to get these out for you, and I'm not able to stay past 5 p.m., especially on Fridays. I have other commitments. Here's what I suggest. Instead of waiting until after your meetings to open the mail, let me open the mail when it arrives at noon and go through the completed contracts. I'll see which ones must be invoiced immediately, and I'll have those on your desk in a file marked PRIORITY. That way you can go through the billings, tell me which ones you want me to invoice, and I can do all that between 3:30 and 4:30 every day. How's that?"

Analysis: What Sandy realized was that her boss wanted a take-charge person. He definitely didn't want a whiner so she kept her feelings about this situation to herself. She acknowledged the importance of getting the invoices out on time, but instead of caving in to all his demands, she offered a solution that ultimately worked for both of them.

Or so she thought.

For the next week or so, Sandy opened up the mail, sorted it, made out the invoices and set aside any letters that she couldn't prioritize. All went well for a few days until Boris began hovering over Sandy's desk, checking and rechecking her work, fearful, Sandy suspected, that she'll make a mistake.

Sandy: *Have I made any mistakes so far?*

Boris: *Not that I'm aware of. Not yet.*

Sandy: *Thank you. So Boris, are you open to a suggestion?*

Boris: *What?*

Sandy: *Let me do my work so that I can finish this in a timely manner and that way you can spend more time on other projects. Give me two weeks to prove this to you, and if I make mistakes, we can decide what to do. If I can do this relatively error-free, then that will make your life so much easier. What do you think?*

Many people in Sandy's position might resort to **feeling** conversations, and that's probably the least effective approach when you're working with a bully. If Sandy moaned, "I can't stand it when you hover over me," or "This micromanaging has got to stop!" Would Boris respond positively? We already heard him criticize Sandy for her complaints.

Some people might just keep doing what they're supposed to do and hold in their feelings until—POP! They explode. Sandy wisely knows not to take that approach. She realized she can't embrace the resistance because she simply does not want to do what her boss tells her to do. But Sandy understands what her boss wants and she treats him the way he wants to be treated. She's emphatic and declarative. Firm and yet caring. THIS is challenging for her because Sandy is not direct and emphatic at all. In fact, she's fairly indirect and extremely sensitive, preferring little or no confrontation at all. She didn't sleep well the night before her conversation with Boris, and it took her hours to drum up the courage to say that speech, but for the five minutes it took for her to make her request, she was able to become who she needed to be. Ultimately, she achieved the outcome she wanted.

Action Steps

In this chapter we've briefly examined some ways to prevent ourselves from "losing it" when we're with unreasonable bosses. Here are some general suggestions from expert writers and authorities.

1. Un-hook. This is a great way to move yourself outside the anger and frustration. Whatever un-hooks you—physical activity, music, dancing, breathing—use it regularly as a method of relieving stress so that you live longer and deal more effectively with idiots.

2. Find out your boss's story first before you speak.

3. Acknowledge the boss's perspective by embracing the resistance. "I can understand why you think that way." "If I were in your shoes, I'd probably make the same decision."

4. Even after acknowledging your boss's point of view, you can bring up objections.
   "Are you open to a suggestion?" "Can I share one other way to look at this?"

5. The conversation with a tough boss can include—in fact—three conversations: What happened? What are you feeling? How does this affect my role here at work?

6. Use alpha breathing. Breathe in through the mouth, out through the nose.

7. Choose a time when you have control over your words...when you can think and speak clearly.

8. Select your words wisely.

9. Speak in very specific, non-punishing terms while you share your story.

10. Detach. Don't take it personally. Refer to or set boundaries that are clear and specific.

And now I have a question for you...

Everyone has a story of the boss from hell, and though I considered a contest to see who had the worst boss in America, I don't want to go there. I would, however, suggest that you go to the Website and point out ways you've succeeded in dealing with "tough" bosses. How do you embrace resistance? What new ways have you invented for dealing more effectively with hard-to-please bosses? What have you specifically done to make tough situations work? Go to the Website (www.themouthtrap.com) and point out ways you've succeeded in dealing with "tough" bosses.

.

Chapter Seven
Coaching Employees From Hell

> *There's only one basic human right: the right to do as you damn well please. And with it comes the only basic human duty, the duty to take the consequences.*
>
> —*P.J. O'Rourke*
>
> *There would be a lot more civility in this world if people didn't take that as an invitation to walk all over you.*
>
> —*Calvin (and Hobbes)*

Though most of us would agree that we work better in an environment in which we feel respected and appreciated, sometimes building a creative organization often includes "socially awkward people" who will, on occasion, "act like assholes." Robert Sutton points out that computer companies who hire geniuses might very well discover that these "creative types" lack people skills, but that's the price we pay sometimes for "out of the box" creativity. Some software manufacturers deliberately hire individuals with anti-social behavior to design iconoclastic video games. When I hired salespeople for my franchise of California Closets decades ago, I deliberately chose hard-to-handle salespeople with a much higher level of dominance than I possessed. I knew full well they would intimidate and irritate me, but at the same time they'd close jobs and increase productivity and profits. They'd "show me the money." Just as we may have to "speak up" to bosses whom we find challenging, we may also have to deal with valuable employees whom we want to keep but who drive us nuts.

The Case of the Whining Pestilence

You're holding a mandatory meeting at work regarding new security policies and procedures added to the employee handbook, and you notice one of the employees is totally disengaged. She's closing her eyes and folding her arms across her chest. When her eyes do finally open, they seem to roll out of their sockets. "Do I have to be here?" she mews and elbows her fellow employee. Obviously bored and ambivalent, she lies back in her chair, shakes her head, puts her arms behind her head, and lets out a loud painful, wrenching groan.

Anyone entering the meeting room now knows Janet doesn't want to be here, and her behavior reflects badly on you because you're holding the meeting.

What are you going to do about it?

Devil's Advocate: Okay, this kind of employee has an attitude problem. I would never let it get this far. No way. No how. We rent people's behavior at work, and this behavior is unacceptable. I'd read her the riot act. I'd tell her to take her car and drive it to the unemployment office because I'm not dealing with this kind inappropriate lazy, ass backwards, attitude.

Dr. Gary: As usual, I think you're overreacting. Let's see what we can do to either "influence" her behavior or establish the right direction for her to go. We certainly don't want her attitude to become infectious or symptomatic of a larger problem. However, if you insult her and say something inappropriate, you may be facing unnecessary consequences. You can always follow discipline procedures. You can, at some point, let her go. Most non-government companies even have "at will" contracts, which means you can quit or be fired, at will. However, why go that route if you want her to stay? Influencing people's behavior—even employees from hell—takes effort. If we can take care of the "problem," we not only rid ourselves of a bad attitude but stop the infection from spreading.

1. First of all, detach and don't let this behavior get to you. It is infantile. People who behave this way want attention. Breathe. Take a break. Unhook. Realize everyone thinks differently. **QTIP** it: **Quit Taking It Personally**. Ask her to step outside.

2. Find out what's going on and set clear limits for this behavior. What's her story? As a manager— no reason why you can't probe first. Did she not get enough sleep? Is she just bored to death? Does she feel this is irrelevant? Acknowledge her perspective and then decide what you want to do. Set your limits. If you want her at the meeting, set up clear boundaries and give her the parameters. And if this behavior is constant, let her know what's acceptable and what's not.

3. Include the content of the three conversations.
   1. What happened?
   2. How does that make you both feel?
   3. And let her know how her attendance fits into her job description.

137

If she says, "This is not part of my job, and I never signed up for this," you have an opportunity to hold an "identity" discussion. What is part of her job and what's not? Let the discussion focus just on that and once you make that clear, ask for her agreement.

4. Decide the appropriate way of conveying this information either through a follow up e-mail, a performance report, a job description, or (least effective) oral commitment.

5. Some offices make this a collaborative effort. Ask for her cooperation. "Help me make this meeting more interesting so that you and others can learn this information quickly and more effectively."

So what might it all look like if you had a discussion with Janet? Here's a sample:

The Coaching Conversation

Fred (the manager) and Janet (the employee)

Fred: I'm not fond of meetings either, but this one is on the benefit package and in 20 minutes you'll learn what's necessary to file the right papers. If you pay attention, it will save you hours of time and questions. Okay?

Janet: Just e-mail me the info.

Fred: That won't work. In fact, I'm going to need your signature that you attended this meeting and that you understood the new rules. If that's something you can't do, let me know right now.

Janet: All right, I'll stay (rolls eyes, folds arms across chest, and huffs and puffs).

Note: But Fred sets clear boundaries. "That won't work." He tells her what he needs, and if necessary he could refer to policies, write her up, and hold her accountable. He's not going there, yet. She sits and cooperates, but still, her body language indicates hostility, and Fred decides to wait before he addresses that again. After the meeting, he asks her into his office. We choose our battles, and Fred decides to take this on.

> **Fred**: *Janet, I want to talk to you about what happened today at the meeting.*
>
> **Janet**: *There's nothing to talk about. You told me I had to stay. I stayed.*
>
> **Fred**: *So if I were an employee walking into that meeting room, and I saw what you did in your seat, what would I have seen?*
>
> **Janet**: *Nothing.*
>
> **Fred**: *Describe to me what you did when you sat down.*
>
> **Janet**: *I just sat down.*
>
> **Fred**: *What did you say to the person sitting next to you?*
>
> **Janet**: *I told her "Another boring meeting."*
>
> **Fred**: *And....*
>
> **Janet**: *I don't know. I just didn't want to be there.*
>
> **Fred**: *How did you make that clear?*
>
> **Janet**: *What are you asking me? Yeah, I probably rolled my eyes and did stuff that showed that I was bored. I mean, can we get on with this? It's 11 a.m. I have stuff to do.*

(Here's the trap: Janet's rudeness may be inappropriate, but if you want to keep her as an employee, put your feelings aside and hunt for the cause of this inappropriate behavior.)

> **Fred**: *So what effect do you think your behavior had on those around you?*
>
> **Janet**: *(No answer)*
>
> **Fred**: *If you saw me doing this (yawning/rolling eyes/expanding chest) what would you think?*

139

Janet: I'd think it's funny.

Fred: Exactly. Would you laugh?

Janet: Yep.

Fred: How's that make you feel—seeing your manager do this while you're talking. What if I did this while you're talking to me (disgusted face)?

(No answer)

Fred: Answer me.

Janet: I guess I'd think it's rude.

Fred: So how do you think I felt when you did what you did? (silence)

Janet: I just can't stand these meetings.

Fred: Did you make that clear to everyone?

Janet: Yes, I guess.

Note: You may be frustrated with how long it takes for Fred to get Janet's acknowledgement that a problem exists, but this has to happen before Fred tries to fix the problem. If Janet doesn't recognize her behavior problem, nothing is going to change.

Fred: Was that behavior appropriate?

Janet: What?

John: I asked you if it was appropriate to let the entire room know that you were bored? If we had a whole group here, and I showed off my disgust for what you're saying, would that be appropriate?

(John stays calm. His voice doesn't waver. He's coaching here.)

John: Janet, you have a right to think and feel what you want but where you share those feelings is an important issue here. So talk to me? Where should you share these issues: publicly or privately?

Janet: I guess privately.

John: *So if you have a problem with these meetings where do you have to go to share your private feelings?*

Janet: *I guess in your office.*

John: *Why didn't you do that?*

Janet: *I don't like talking to you. You just don't seem to care. I work here, and I have to tell you I just don't feel appreciated. I think you talk down to me. Like right now I feel like I'm back in grade school again.*

Fred: *Well, forgive me if I am making you feel that way. I'm just asking you questions and I'm learning two things. A. You hate meetings. B. You don't like talking to me about it because you feel I talk down to you. I'd like to change both those things, Fair?*

Janet: *I guess.*

Fred: *You're an important part of the department, and I don't want to lose you. I do want you to discuss things you're upset about with me privately–in an office— rather than share those feelings visibly at meetings, unless it's appropriate. If you're willing to do that, I'm willing to be a better listener. What do you say?*

The line in the sand has been drawn. If Janet's negative behavior continues, Fred can choose to fire her, write her up, or continue to persuade her to get help. If Janet agrees to change her behavior, then Fred has to follow up on that. He can train her himself or send her to a training program and follow up on any changes that she makes.

The coaching formula from Ferdinand F. Fournies' *Coaching for Improved Work Performance* looks like this:

1. Find out the problem.
2. Agree that the problem exists.
3. Negotiate a solution.
4. Follow up to make sure the person follows the solution.

5. Recognize the changed behavior and show appreciation.

The whole purpose of having a "coaching" conversation is to unearth the problem. If you can get Janet to recognize what the problem is, you can then decide on a solution, but if you can't get to a point where the employee recognizes the problem, nothing will change.

You can see from the tone of the conversation how easy it is to sound demeaning. Sometimes when we share information that is simple, we tend to sound like grade school teachers. There are some ways to avoid this.

1. Let the employee know from the start you'll have coaching conversations that will ask questions. That's just the way we work here.
2. Make certain you sound empathetic. Practice your voicing.
3. Decide what outcome you want before you coach. If necessary, create a mutual outcome. "We both want to work this out, right?"
4. Be absolutely 100-percent sincere.

In the previous conversation, Fred wants Janet to stay. He doesn't want her to quit, and he doesn't want to fire her. He does, however, want to change the attitude, and that is one of the most challenging tasks employers endure when dealing with difficult employees.

And now I have a question for you...

Gossip is a common behavior we see in most offices, and, whereas the behavior described above can be documented and anticipated through policies and procedures, gossip is much more nebulous. How do you control a steady stream of backstabbing, opinion-making, and grumbling?

In one department at a high school, a team of teachers, who have taught for years, eat lunch every day and unfortunately their "gossip" about other teachers filters through the department down the corridors to the department chair and principal. Several new teachers have complained and transferred to other schools (pay is the same) just so that they work in friendlier environments. You can't fire this "clique" of teachers because they're tenured. So as a communication professional, what can you do to change the environment so that it remains more positive and open? Share your answers, as always, on the mouth trap Website.

Chapter Eight

Maybe You Didn't Say a Word, but Your Body Language Gave You Away

> *Studies show that when negotiating over the telephone, the person with the stronger argument usually wins, but this is not so true when negotiating face-to-face, because, overall, we make final decisions [based] more on what we see than what we hear.*
>
> —Allan and Barbara Pease
>
> *Think of the people who command presence every time they enter a room. What do they do that makes people respond to them?*
>
> —Susan Bixler and Lisa Scherrer Dugan

First Impressions

One late afternoon, I bumped into a neighbor while retrieving my mail from the common mail boxes in our townhouse complex.

"You're the mean guy who drives the Mustang, right?" he asked.

Mean guy?

"I see you drive into the complex sometimes," my neighbor continued. "The top's down, and you have a scowl on your face like you're ready to bite someone's head off."

"Hey, I'm the nicest guy in the world."

"Could have fooled me. I thought of introducing myself a few years ago, but I wasn't sure you'd be the kind of person I'd want to meet." He laughed.

"So did I surprise you?" I responded.

In most business encounters, we have a few seconds to form a first impression. Before a word is spoken, people take note of our physical presence—posture, a handshake, eye contact—and draw immediate conclusions. My neighbor, for example, didn't make an effort to meet me because he assumed, from my demeanor, that I had a mean streak. Our subsequent meetings changed that impression. We soon discovered we had much in common—we're both speakers and writers—and during the next couple of weeks we e-mailed each other ideas, networked, and eventually met for lunch. Had I not had the opportunity to talk to him, I might have remained "unapproachable," based on what he saw of me driving into our complex.

Consider this: How do people perceive you both at work and at home? Our bodies generate energy on many levels. People perceive anger, frustration, confusion, incompetence, competence, or strength just by looking at us.

However, these early perceptions are not always accurate, as I discovered that afternoon.

According to experts, we have the most control over our facial muscles. That may be partly because "the hardest areas of our body to control are those farthest away from (the) brain—that is hands and feet," says Gregory Hartley in *How to Spot a Liar.*

If you've ever had to endure a confrontational conversation and you didn't want to be there—does your body language give away your true feelings? You may go in with a "straight face" but the leg shakes, the hands steeple, the finger tips touch your chin, the pupils become smaller, and when you get defensive, you may even resort to "batoning," the act of using your arm to emphasize a point (a gesture Hitler used when whipping the populace into shape).

Many times we aren't conscious of the body betraying our thoughts. We may fold both arms across our chest because we're cold but be perceived as arrogant and distant. We may scratch our head because the dandruff itches, but others view us as confused. We yawn, but not because we're bored or tired. We just yawn. We may even wring our hands, play with a ballpoint pen, or tap the table purely out of habit, not because we're nervous. And yet, people draw conclusions immediately from what they see.

Let's take a quick stroll down the hallway of a typical company:

"Bill's not getting anything done. He's gazing into space."

"Marjorie always seems so angry. Look at that scowl."

"Look at him. He's laughing. He doesn't give a hoot about what just happened."

"Phil must be talking to his boss. Look at the way he shakes his head, rolls his eyes. Wait. As soon as we pass by, he'll throw his arms in the air. See!"

Yikes! Are we that predictable?

David Allen says, "You won't see how to do it until you see yourself doing it."

Videotape yourself and have others watch the tape with you. In one viewing, pay attention to the verbal content and in another viewing examine just the body language.

Years ago, when I videotaped one of my first speaking engagements, I discovered I swayed back and forth as if I were on a ship afloat a rocky sea. I also snapped my fingers too much and rarely moved around. After seeing my video-tape, I changed those habits immediately, and it wasn't very difficult because *I saw exactly* what didn't work and made the appropriate changes.

147

Here are some strategies and tips for taking control over your body language so that you create the right impression from the very start of a conversation.

SOFTEN

How do we position ourselves so we are *not* betrayed by body fatigue? How do we create the power pose or a more relaxed stance that will get us the outcome we want on a regular basis?

Let's look at the SOFTEN key components that create presence.

Smile: Had I smiled instead of grimaced in the car, I would have created an entirely different image of myself. I think we'd all look silly grinning in our cars on Los Angeles freeways, but a conscious effort to smile when you walk into someone's office suggests an open, friendly, warm attitude. Note: Spontaneous, genuine smiles are symmetrical. Deliberately planned smiles are cocked slightly to the side of the mouth.

Open: When you have a conversation, an open stance suggests you're willing to listen. Your arms are not folded, often stationed at one side, palms up. Open palms suggest honesty and approval. A wave of the arm—"Come on in"—or standing up when someone walks into an office will present a welcoming presence.

Frontal lean is a simple gesture. You lean forward (rather than back) to suggest you're there for that person. But leaning forward with hands on both knees, or with both hands gripping the chair, might be construed as overly anxious: You're ready to terminate the conversation.

Touch: Touching a person with your left hand while shaking hands with your right can be powerful. Elbow and hand touching, when done discreetly, grabs attention. However, listen to your gut instincts and recognize the environment. Not everyone wants to have their shoulder touched or feel hugged, or for that matter even approached. If you're conscious of the other person's body language, you can decide how close to get. If in doubt, leave it out.

Note: Some people prefer not to shake hands because of the exchange of bacteria. However, reaching out to shake someone's hand is a normal, professional connection in American business. Avoiding that gesture may signify distrust or an aloof attitude.

Eye contact: This is one of the most powerful ways to create rapport. Some experts say it's best to look above the eyes so you're not staring into the other person's pupils, because not every culture appreciates direct eye contact. In Asian societies, looking someone straight in the eye is not polite, but in American business, eye movement can make or break rapport. People appreciate the attention.

Nod: A "nod" not only indicates you're listening; it encourages the other person to give you more information. According to Alan Pease, "Head nodding encourages cooperation and agreement." Men nod differently than women do. A woman may nod and that means "I'm following you," but if you ask her if she agrees, she may shake her head. For men, the nod might imply both meanings: "I'm following you and I agree with you."

You should also pay attention to your leg, arm, and hand movements.

Arm and hand movements: People with power don't have to gesticulate too much. "Use clear, uncomplicated, deliberate movements," says Pease. The faster and more erratic your movements, the more difficult it is for people to engage.

Leg movement: Men should keep their legs together in business meetings, particularly when speaking with women. A woman, of course, will feel intimidated by a man who keeps his legs wide apart during a business encounter. This is partly because women don't feel comfortable mirroring that position.

Shaking one's leg, folding the legs, tapping a foot, straddling a chair—these motions detract from an image of power, so be conscious of body parts that are furthest from the brain. Even leaning back with arms behind the head (sometimes dubbed the pistol-shooting position) is often considered relaxed aggressiveness. "Okay. I'm ready. Spill your guts."

The best piece of advice from experts? Match your physical presence to the outcome you want.

> *"My favorite moment in business was the day I got fired. I walked into Bill's office, and he was as sweet and patient as a puppy dog. I'm telling you, he came off as my bud. Soft eyes. Caring voice. He angled his chair so that he'd face me. Then he leaned over, looked me in the eye, took my hand, and fired me. I was never so surprised in my life. If I had been firing him, I would have been shaking in my boots. My voice would have trembled. I would have cried and made that poor person scared out of his mind. But, I'll have to say, his self-assuredness calmed me down and he said, with complete conviction, that I deserve a job where I can be myself. And I believed him. I hated that job. I just did everything I could to type those memos and file those folders, and every day I resented being there. So it was not just his voice but his physical presence that let me know, it was okay to leave. I will be just fine. "*
>
> —Lucille Ackerman, a struggling comic

Steps for Creating the Power Pose

- ➢ Sit straight.
- ➢ Look people in the eye.

> Videotape yourself so you can catch any ticks or movements that detract from your message.

> Be present, always.

> Use a mirror when you speak on the phone. Be cognizant of times when you're upset or angry. If you don't want those emotions expressed, adjust the thought and then adjust the look.

> Anchor yourself with the "thought" that will best help you succeed during a particular encounter: "I am making my point and getting the outcome I want." "I am giving Lucille an opportunity to recharge her life. This job is not for her. She will find a better one."

> Breathe in through the nose, out through the mouth, and calm yourself before you have a difficult conversation.

> Before you meet with a hard-to-please customer or employee, "stage" your physical presence. Visualize how you want to look so the body will match your mind.

Devil's Advocate: *Hold on, hold on one second. Are you giving acting lessons here? I never heard anything so crazy in my life. I'm the CEO of a huge software firm. I am who I am. I put my cards on the table. I don't wear a mask. I leave that for liars and masqueraders.*

Dr. Gary: *So when you hear bad news, do you wear that on your sleeve?*

Devil's Advocate: *Sometimes.*

Dr. Gary:And when you negotiate and feel excited when you see the other side reducing their prices, do you get all giddy and emotional? Do you say "Whoopee?"

You think it but you don't act it.

Devil's Advocate: What's your point?

Dr. Gary: That's acting. We do it every day. We become who we need to be. Sometimes it's less apparent than other times. Occasionally, we just "breathe" and "think" before we speak. Other times, we visualize ourselves as steel warriors able to deal with anything that comes our way. Tony Robbins calls this neuro-linguistic-programming, and this "change of thought," discussed in **Chapter 3** *will influence how we look, how we behave, and how we are perceived. I bet Howard Dean wishes he had better control over his body language when he announced to millions of Americans his desire to "take Ohio!"*

If we believe what we're doing is the right thing, our bodies will stay in tune with our thoughts. If we believe what we're doing is the wrong thing, our bodies may betray us. So before you have any conversation, check your thoughts at the door and physically prepare yourself.

When Body Language Betrays Our Thoughts

Certainly if we draw conclusions based on a quick glance inside someone's cubicle or office, as we saw earlier, we will often misread people. We can't always match "content" with "body language" so we make erroneous assumptions based on a snapshot view. We see someone with slumped shoulders, eyes to the floor, and we think—Loser! But that person might be reacting to an e-mail he just read about layoffs. Had we read that same e-mail, we might have responded the same way.

The solution?

Close your door. People are watching!

Make a conscious effort to be aware of how you're perceived so you aren't misjudged or pigeonholed.

The trap we fall into is twofold:

First, we allow the body to subvert our thoughts. We don't want to give an indication anything's wrong, but no matter how hard we try, people can tell something's the matter.

"Gary, what's wrong?"

"Nothing."

"No really, what's going on?"

The second dilemma is even more complicated and surreal. We pretend to be something we're not. We take on a job we think we can do, but we innately know it's not our thing. No matter how hard we try to be positive, the thought buried in our brains release chemical flows to the body and we slump, we tilt our heads down, and our facial muscles sag. Even when we try to put on a "public" face, our bodies often deceive us.

Ever go into a meeting or a confrontation that you instinctively know won't go your way? *It won't go my way.* That thought wears on you—mind, face, arms, and legs. Susan Scotty says, "If your behavior contradicts your values, your body knows and you pay a price at a cellular level."

Some people are better at pretending than others. Obviously, in politics (as in acting), one can learn to put on a good show. But how many times have you heard people say things like this?

153

"You don't want to be here, do you? Uh…you sure this is good time?"

"I know exactly what you're thinking. Me too. I feel the same way."

"Are we in trouble here? I see you're unhappy."

"You just gave me this look, and I have to tell you, I'm scared. I mean I'm really scared 'cause if you don't want to be here, then what the hell am I doing here?"

"Not good news, huh?"

"So you're upset about something. Talk to me."

"I didn't do it… honestly."

People filled with doom and despair—negaholics!—often wear pessimism on their faces and shoulders. People who seek recognition, acknowledgment, and acceptance, similarly allow their bodies to exude positive energy:

Look at that guy. He's so together. How does he work effectively under so much pressure? Remarkable!

Sometimes greatness is defined by how well people deal with confrontation, stress, anxiety, and manipulation. It's certainly one of the key questions we ask when we interview people. How will they function under stress? Are they approachable? Non-approachable? If you're hoping to hire someone who will calmly—with great poise—handle difficult situations, then what would that look like? This is probably not a difficult question to answer. We can see on television almost every day how individuals respond under pressure, and we remember the awkward, nervous moments. The reaction shots—a stare, a rolling of the eyes, a shaking of the head—from politicians responding to a comment made by one of their adversaries. At the same time, we also recognize the importance of preparing both thoughts, tone, and body language so that the image we create is the one we want.

"The easiest way to practice this," a colleague once shared with me, "is to check yourself at the door. Decide who you want to be. Look at yourself in the mirror before you walk in the room or simply close your eyes, visualize the posture, and act the part."

How to Deal With Other People's Body Language

What happens, though, when the person you're speaking to gives off vibes you find disagreeable? How should we deal with other people's body language?

You walk into a room and your manager is typing in front of his computer.

"Hey, what's up?" he asks.

"I just need a few moments of your time."

"Fine. I'm all yours," the manager replies, but he never looks up. His fingers remain on the keys, and he steadfastly focuses on what he has to do. The message comes through loud and clear. *What you say is not as important as my typing.*

How do we deal with that?

Let's examine this particular dilemma from both perspectives:

From the interrupter's point of view

1. Probe first to see if this is a good time.

2. If it isn't, then re-schedule your discussion. Most people can't put two thoughts into their heads at the same time. If this is an emergency, point out the importance of full comprehension. What's in it for the listener to stop what he's doing and listen? Make that clear and ask for a few minutes of uninterrupted time.

It might go like this:

"Boss, what I have to say is important. Is this a good time?"

"This is fine. I'm just trying to finish this contract." (type type type)

"I would appreciate it if I could have your undivided attention for five minutes so we can solve this problem and not have to deal with it later. It's very important. Okay?"

From the perspective of the person being interrupted

1. Position yourself to listen. Put your stuff aside and listen 100 percent.

2. Instead of "pretending" to listen, be honest and share your concerns. "I have so much work to do. Can we talk about this later?"

3. Follow SOFTEN and be fully present.

4. "I only have a few minutes. Is that enough?" And keep control over the meeting so you don't feel your time's wasted.

5. If you have stuff on your mind, "stake" it. That is, take a few moments to write it down so it won't be in your head. You will then be more open to listening.

In the previous example, the manager was simply trying to multi-task, a common occurrence in work today.

But what if our intentions are slightly more toxic?

Toxic Example: You meet with another employee and you can tell, from the slightly drawn, angular, angry expression on her face that she's unhappy. Yet she says: "I'm so glad you're here. Let's get started." As the conversation continues, she looks at her watch, half-grins, or stands up occasionally and opens the door to see if her next appointment is there.

Match the thought with the body language. *Though you can't read this woman's thoughts, you assume from her body language, that she's disinterested and anxious for you to leave.*

When you leave, she says, "I'll get back to you."

Deep in your soul, you know darn well you'll never hear from her again.

People sense when you're sincere and when you're not, and that incongruence bothers them.

The same incongruence works with tone of voice. Susan Scott points out that when we truly listen to people, we want to hear exactly what they say (listen for content), what they're feeling (listen for emotion), and what they're truly going to do (listen for intent). "We're going to get to that project right away" might be said in a flip tone of voice, with sarcasm, or in a belligerent manner. Re-translated, the words might mean: "Get off my back!"

Ambivalence, disgust, frustration, and misunderstanding can be inferred by the mere furl of an eyebrow, the shake of our heads, the rolling of ours eyes, a fingertip touching the chin. One of the common complaints I hear is that people don't know where they stand. They work with others and feel an overriding sense of doom.

Some suggestions:

> ➤ Question them: "Sally, I realize I might be off base here, but are you mad at me? Did I do something wrong?"

> ➤ Call them on it: "It seems to me you're annoyed. Am I right? Let's talk about it." Or, "I'm sensing a disconnect here. I know you said you wanted to work together, but you also seem frustrated. Talk to me. What's going on?"

> ➤ Observe the entire picture. Remember, a raised eyebrow doth not tell the whole story. Base your observation on the complete "context" of a situation including tone, the actual words, and a series of gestures.

Devil's Advocate: An interesting alternative to "live" conversations or "phone" conversations is texting or e-mails. I find that instead of interrupting someone or dealing with the rudeness we might expect, we can send a text message or an e-mail that can be read leisurely and responded to at that person's convenience. Hence, no fear of body language. In fact, I recommend we avoid live conversations entirely because they prove to be full of hidden ticks and eye movement and body language that simply get in the way. You want me to do something? E-mail or text me. I'll get back to you when I can.

Dr. Gary: On one level, I agree. A text message asking me to deliver papers at a certain date will take less time than a visit into my office. Also, if that visit interrupts my work, it will take awhile to regain focus. I'm starting to like the efficiency of text message/e-mail over live conversations. But give me a break: When you limit your communication to writing, you're playing with fire, because anything you put in writing could ultimately land you in jail. See Chapter 10 on e-mail road rage.

Avoiding live encounters is highly impractical, but we are indeed moving toward technology-based communication. Is sending an e-mail easier? Would you prefer leaving a 5 p.m. voicemail so that you don't have to speak to the person? Many people prefer these options. That's partly because it takes such work, preparation, talent, and courage to make a "live" message pure, untainted, and 100 percent understood.

Action Steps

1. Create presence by being conscious of your power pose.

2. Be aware of how others read you. What do you look like? What nervous ticks to do you have? Do you shake your leg? Is it difficult to look someone in the eye? Do a body language MRI on yourself by videotaping a conversation or a speech.

3. Before disconnecting from a speaker, be aware that your perception may not be what that person is presenting. Probe first.

4. To fully understand body language, interconnect all the symbols. Look at the whole story—verbal, tone, and body language—and then draw your conclusions.

And now I have a question for you...

A year or two out of architecture school, Jorge had dinner with Larson Smith, an old buddy of his dad's and a successful architect. Jorge looked forward to this meeting for months, but when the two of them finally met, Larson spent half of the time talking on his cell phone. Even while Jorge spoke about his ambitions, the man's attention drifted. The only time Larson seemed fully engrossed was when the bill came and Jorge offered to pick up the tab. Larson did little to protest.

Jorge told me later, "He said he enjoyed meeting me and promised to see what he could do for me in terms of finding a job, but he wasn't invested. I dismissed it and said, 'Can't win over everyone.' And yet, this was a family friend who disconnected from me on almost every level, and I will never forgive him."

If Jorge drummed up his courage and spoke to his mentor in the parking lot outside the restaurant, what might he say?

Chapter Nine

The Diversity Chapter

Free Yourself From Jokes, Sidebars, and Offensive Remarks That Lead to Trouble

Coworker: So what do you call a bunch of Asians in a swimming pool?

Rhonda: (Shrugs shoulders). I'm late for a meeting.

Coworker: Cup-of-noodle!

Rhonda: (ignores joke)

Coworker: Cup-of-noodle! I thought that was a funny joke.

Rhonda: (Looking perplexed). Sorry, are we saying all Asians eat Cup-of-Noodles? Why is that funny?

Coworker: Lots of Asian people eat noodles. It's just a joke.

Rhonda: I eat noodles. I'm not Asian.

Coworker: Oh come on. I see many of the secretaries eating Ramen. George thought the joke was funny.

Rhonda: Well tell it to Linda. She's from Taiwan. See if she finds it funny. She's standing right over there.

Coworker: No, thank you. Never mind. I was just trying to make a joke.

If you've ever been in a situation where you feel uncomfortable, even unsafe, after someone tells a racist joke, you could, as Carmen Van Kerckhove suggests in her blog, "How to Respond to a Racist Joke," play dumb and ask the person to explain the joke. That way, she says, "You are able to draw the racist stereotype out into the open, address it directly, and demonstrate how absurd and offensive it is."

You could also simply *not* laugh. Just walk away. However, a private conversation like the previous one or a dialogue like the one that follows could put an end to the joke-telling behavior and save the culprit from harassment charges.

Manager: John, I'd be careful telling those jokes at work. If I found it offensive, then so will other people, and you could get in trouble. The company policy spells out these rules, and we'll cover them in the training program.

John: I was just repeating this funny joke from TV, and you're reading me the riot act?

Manager: Federal and State law says we have the right to work in a safe environment and people who tell offensive jokes violate both our company policy and the law.

John: But it's only a joke. I repeated what a comedian said on the David Letterman show!

Manager: I understand. It wouldn't matter if you heard it on Howard Stern, Jay Leno, or your favorite sitcom. The media has different boundaries. Inside this company we have specific boundaries that control free speech and the kinds of humor, sarcasm, jokes, and quips we can tell. Our training class will outline these requirements, but I can sum up the rule in three words.

John: *Okay. (Pause) What are those words?*

Manager: *Don't do it. Just don't tell those jokes. It's not worth the grief, hassle and potential damage it can cause you and others. I'm not saying we can't laugh and have a good time. But if you think a joke might offend someone, leave it out. Agreed?*

But...Humor in the Workplace Increases Productivity

It's a difficult challenge for many of us for a variety of reasons. According to Daniel Goleman, author and expert on emotional intelligence, jokes and laughter help to "stimulate employee creativity and improve communication and trust." Casual conversation and humor during a negotiation may even help "increase the likelihood of financial concessions." We also recognize the healing power of comedy. Humor not only releases stress, studies have shown that laughter can improve one's physical and mental health, reduce pain, enhance the immune system and create a healthier outlook on life. The trap we fall into is when the humor bypasses our mental detectors and disengages the audience: Instead of healing, the humor hurts, damages, infects, offends, and even harasses the listener. In an age in which the boundaries are often limitless on satellite radio, cable stations, and movies, it's often tough to know where to draw the line and keep ourselves from sharing the occasional "slip of the tongue" or sarcastic remark.

The law says that any joke that is "severe or pervasive" enough to create a hostile or abusive work environment or is based on race, sex, religion, national origin, or several other protected categories, can be deemed harassment. Whether it's sexual suggestive pictures, jokes, slurs, or personal insults, most experts recommend employers institute a "no tolerance policy" because in the workplace today, bigoted/racist/sexual humor can lead to law suits and hefty damage awards.

So when people say—"Oh, you gotta hear this joke." *(No you don't. Save it for after work).*

"I shouldn't be telling you this, but…." *(Stop them! Do them a favor! If your first instincts are to withhold, withhold!)*

"I'm going to send you via e-mail the list of highway signs I just got. Hysterical. Each one suggests a different sexual position." *(No thank you. Don't fax, download, mail, send, or pass along. Leave those visual jokes at home.)*

"Did you see the movie that opened Friday? Could you believe what those girls did? Oh my God. Especially in that one scene when…." *(Frank, save it for happy hour.)*

Obviously, my three words, "Don't do it," hardly seems embedded in the national consciousness of millions of American business professionals. Not a day goes by when we don't hear some individual, a political candidate, or celebrity say a remark that gets them into trouble. One supposes that if a remark can nearly topple the career of a comedian, a presidential candidate, a coach for a national football team or a highly successful disk jockey, then how do average Americans cope? How do we learn to curb remarks we instinctively want to share even if we suspect they might be deemed inappropriate in the workplace?

Here are some specific challenges I've heard across the country and suggestions for addressing them.

Become a Human Benchmark

A group of bank managers, all men, each wearing matching polo shirts with the bank's insignia embroidered on the pocket, sit in the lobby coffee shop of a Los Angeles office building. While sipping lattes, they tell raunchy jokes, one of which is about an overweight hooker.

The server, a hefty woman in her late 50s, has heard worse jokes in the past, but this one seems particularly tasteless and insensitive, and the group's laughter ultimately gets on her nerves. She thinks she should say something and then decides not to, but when the bank president comes in for coffee that afternoon, she drums up the courage and shares with him her thoughts. "I wasn't going to say anything, but...." and she describes her frustration regarding some of the rude behavior and unseemly jokes she often hears from the bank personnel. "They're a good group, and I hate to say anything that would put them in trouble, but I didn't need to hear another fat joke this morning!"

By the end of the day, the president calls the five managers into the office, admonishes each of them for their lack of discretion, including their supervisor, Ed, who wasn't even present during any of the joke-telling sessions. Ed knew, however, this behavior was going on and never said anything to stop it.

At a meeting later that week, many members of the staff protested, saying it was unfair to punish employees for telling jokes and having fun on their breaks outside work.

But here's what the president said:

"We live in a free country. I can't create a policy limiting the kinds of things we talk about when you're not working. A few jokes here and there—no big deal. What I object to, however, is simple: When you walk outside the bank, on bank hours, wearing the bank uniforms, you represent the company, and anything that pours out of your mouths that might be deemed disrespectful or demeaning could damage not only your reputation but that of the company's.

"If you were in the waiting room of an office and you overheard the HR director telling a racist, sexist, anti-Semitic, or fat joke just before he opens the door to interview you, would

165

you want to work there? People do get a negative impression of who we are by the insensitivity we show to others, and I think it's important to keep all that in mind when you tell a joke. That's it."

Though most of the group nodded their heads, one shrugged his shoulders and protested.

"I don't see what the problem is. It was just a joke. Alice (the server) has heard us tell jokes before, and I've seen her laugh. The joke wasn't told to her. We were telling it to each other. What are we supposed to do? Not talk during our breaks?"

The president paused, scratched his head. "Alice, the waitress at the coffee shop on the ground floor, felt embarrassed and humiliated by dozens of your jokes; this is just the first time she's said anything. I think as bank managers, we want to be remembered for the dreams we provide and the savings we create—not a crass, humiliating joke that might hurt someone's feelings.

"So this is the rule, and though I'm not sure I can legally enforce it outside the physical boundaries of this bank, I am asking each and every one of you to be role models. Tell jokes. Be funny. If you have the slightest doubt that a joke or a reference you use might offend anyone, leave it out. Can you do that for me?"

A few jokes may not cause a law suit, but most workers would probably agree that if telling a raunchy joke may be deemed inappropriate and cause disciplinary action, why take the risk? Our mission? We simply must strive for class and professionalism. Who do we want to be? How do we want to be perceived? "In every society, there are 'human benchmarks,'" Dan Sullivan says in *The Strategic Coach*. "Certain individuals whose behavior becomes a model for everyone—stirring examples that others admire and emulate." Comedy, by its very nature, puts down, mocks, and satirizes others, so telling jokes at work inherently means you're taking risks.

When I tell a joke, will it be appreciated in such a way that I'm not offending anyone? That is the question we have to answer every time we feel compelled to open our mouth and be funny at the workplace. And, for some of us, it is difficult to control that impulse to utter a sarcastic or off-color remark that we might think is hysterical. Why do we do it? Is it that we want to show off? Does it truly illustrate a point? Are we competing for a role we once had in school—class clown?

Place Your Humor (In the Right Place)

The supervisor at a local market told me recently, "Look, I love racy humor. I used to sit in my room and listen to my dad's Red Foxx albums. Even now I always have Sirius satellite radio turned to the raunchy joke channel. If I had the money, I might even treat myself to a night at the Improv and hear comedians try out their material, but when I hear that same humor in the backroom of my market, I cringe because I know not everyone appreciates those jokes like I do, and one complaint could lead to hundreds of thousands of dollars of legal fees.

"Ever see two people swooning and kissing in public? You just want to turn to them and say, 'GET A ROOM!' I feel the same way about racy/sexist/ethnic joke-telling. Take it home with you. Don't tell it near the asparagus."

So the decision here is easy.

According to EEOC guidelines, (Equal Employment Opportunity Commission), "Few judges extend constitutional protection to speech that causes a hostile work environment."

If in doubt, leave it out.

But so many of us tell the joke and then apologize afterwards. "You know I'm just joking…" "Did I say that? Wow! I can't believe those words just plopped out of my mouth." Bill Maher on HBO's *Real Time with Bill Maher* will make a jabbing cruel remark that incites the audience to boo, and then

167

follow it with, "I kid here...." but that's cable TV, a no-holds-bar zone, and you pay to watch shows that include adult content, nudity, and violence. I don't believe that a sign is plastered above the lunchroom of your corporate headquarters warning you that you are entering a "raunchy humor" zone. When we're caught in the crossfire of a demeaning sexist joke, we feel trapped. *Hey, it's just a joke!* As we well know, though, jokes are key indicators of a person's prejudices and insensitivity. All humor is rooted in truth, and if we hear someone's insulting comments, we start distancing ourselves from that individual. The distance leads to distrust, then anger, frustration, even hostility.

Devil's Advocate: Yes, but. Why can't I just be me? In fact, people know what to expect from me. I tell it like it is, and they appreciate that. I'm the life of the party.

Dr Gary: Are you? Sometimes curmudgeons, like yourself, aren't even aware of how their humor rubs people the wrong way. We are more quotable than we think. People may not always bravely speak up (like Rhonda in the earlier example). They may say nothing publicly, but privately they may complain. A racist joke could prove to be so offensive that you may end up months later defending your beliefs in a closed door session or in a court of law.

Be Careful Who You Are, on and off the Stage

Consider this: One of my favorite motivational speakers, someone I had admired for years, speaks at a luncheon. Though not everyone may agree with his conservative politics, he's a riveting, highly entertaining speaker who frequently refers to his complete devotion to his wife of 48 years and to his large (and growing) family. He has 19 grandchildren!

After hearing him speak at this luncheon, I happened to see him in the bathroom. We were washing our hands and he turned to me, a perfect stranger, and commented on the Notre Dame Football game—he hopes they'll beat USC—and the beautiful woman who introduced him. "Isn't she the hottest thing you've ever seen? I'd like to screw her all night long until my teeth get dizzy."

The image itself—dizzy teeth—stuck with me for hours. No, years.

It's not that I'm a prude. It just took me by surprise—happily married for 48 years—19 grandchildren—my mentor! My mentor, author of books on positive thinking, a healer, a proponent for integrity, truth, and ethics in the workplace!

"Say it ain't so!"

It's even hard for me to listen to one of his CDs now without being reminded of "Dizzy teeth" and what I guess you would call his implicit hypocrisy.

A few minutes ago he was preaching to us the power of commitment, the necessity for *values* in our lives, and off stage he obviously didn't hold true to those beliefs.

Be careful of who you are on and off stage. If you invite people back to your house, what you say and the environment you create are an indication of who you really are.

How am I perceived by others? Do I care? If I do, watch the words I use, the jokes I tell.

Just as the server at the coffee shop dubbed those bank managers insensitive and rude, we hear a comment that we deem inappropriate and it influences our first impressions.

Devil's Advocate: No, no, no, no, no. I hear what you're saying about "placing" jokes at work. But I have to argue with your premise regarding Mr. Motivational Speaker. What's the big deal? What he does off stage is really none of your business.

Dr. Gary: A motivational speaker sets himself up as a role model. If he is going to tell the audience one thing ("I am devoted to my wife") and do the opposite off stage, his values seem not only corrupted but artificial. His words now lack meaning. Managers and supervisors are role models, and if they expect their staff members to be respectful and authentic, they must lead by example.

Devil's Advocate: But you know, I can't always control what I have to say. Sometimes words spill out, and by the time the words roll off the tongue, it is too late to retract.

Dr. Gary: That is not exactly true with jokes or sidebars. The motivational speaker "chose" to share a thought with me; the words didn't just spill out. He could have held his thoughts safely in his head. Was it that he trusted me? Did he just have this urgent need to be "raw" for a couple of minutes? I don't know, but he'd have been much better off not sharing it.

When you're at work, be the most professional class act you can be.

Be clear what your intentions are and if you are in doubt as to what is appropriate, say nothing. The benefits are enormous. People not only feel safe working around you, but when you're able to communicate with larger groups on a regular basis, you earn the respect of people inside and outside your circle of influence. When people know that you have the ability to say the right thing, they'll rely on your expertise, pay you more money, and promote you to positions in which they know you'll proceed with intelligence and caution. Having said that, here are a few more specific traps people fall into that often cause humiliation, shame, and embarrassment.

Am I off-kilter here or do men seem to deliver more aggressive humor than women?

Admittedly, all the embarrassing and humiliating examples I've included in this chapter came from men. Why is that? According to an interview David Shipley and Will Schwalbe conducted with Deborah Tanen in their book *Send*, men and women inherently have diverse conversational styles. Perhaps more sensitive to other person's emotions, women are less likely to joke than men. Men, for example, are more likely to send teasing, sarcastic jokes via e-mail, and male humor, in general, tends to be of a more violent, aggressive nature. Comedienne and English professor Regina Barreca suggests that most women don't like aggressive, physical, knuckle-in-your-face humor like you'd see in a "three Stooges" film. "Eye-poking, butt-slamming humor—we don't do that. Some Men use insulting humor to bond and insult each other." The example she gives is that you can tease a man for wearing a 30-year-old jacket, and he may proudly explain how much money he's saved, but if you tease a woman about her old, unfashionable dress ("Did you buy that at a garage sale?") she'll never speak to you again.

Rarely, if ever, do you hear of cases in which men sue women for abusive humor. It's usually the other way around, so the message to men seems clearly obvious:

171

You're much better off just leaving any kind of aggressive, pandering, seemingly off-kilter humor at home. It will only get you into trouble, and you don't want to get your eye poked out.

Is it all right for someone to tell jokes about their own group (that is, Polish people tell Polish jokes, blondes tell blonde jokes)?

I don't think it matters who tells the story. If it's still going to offend someone else, don't tell it. Also, self-deprecating humor backfires much of the time. An accountant reacts when one of her employees complains about the busy work balancing the books. "Well what do you want from me, I'm Jewish. I want every cent accounted for."

Not only might the joke not be funny, but it stereotypes and pigeonholes a behavior in a most unflattering way. The manager could have a legitimate reason for asking employees to pore over every number. Blaming it on his Jewish heritage is inaccurate and disparaging.

I once got in trouble for hiring someone to speak at a conference and her jokes were insulting and inappropriate. How do we avoid that? I'm not a mind reader. How should I know what jokes she'll tell?

In terms of placement, it is not a bad idea to investigate the material before it is presented or "placed" at a meeting or a convention. Even if you hire a comedian for a conference or you ask someone to prepare some introductory words at an award celebration, be careful of any material that may offend your audience.

Years ago a friend of mine told me a story that has since become somewhat legendary in Los Angeles. Here's what happened:

The chairperson of entertainment for a convention in West Los Angeles hired a local stage company to do scenes from a play as part of the big dinner dance. She had heard the play was well received by LA critics, and she was able to hire the actors for nearly nothing so that they could publicize their play and their new theatre.

Once the dinner and awards were over, the curtain went up, and there was, in full uniform, a dominatrix slapping and whipping a half naked man in a chair while demanding him to recite a pledge of loyalty.

Seeing this, the entertainment director stormed onto stage and pulled down the curtain, her voice several octaves higher than usual. "You'll have to excuse the players," she said, stuttering. "Ah, they must have...not realized where they were performing, and ah...well I'm just going to apologize."

The truth was that this red faced chairperson assumed the play, Jean Genet's *The Balcony*—which got rave reviews from local critics—was of a certain moral caliber (she thought it was about a "balcony") and had refused to check it out ahead of time or delegate someone to see or read the play first. She could have just apologized, but instead she did something that ennobled her to all who attended that particular dinner.

She took full responsibility for the fiasco.

The next day, she recorded a message that went out on the voice mails of nearly two hundred attendees: "I did a stupid thing today, and I wanted to share it with you. I didn't investigate something that I knew nothing about. That was dumb, and I will be much more careful next time." Due to her honest, apologetic attitude, her organization laughed at the incident (for years!), and she turned what could have been a truly humiliating incident into one of the funniest evenings the banking community will remember for a long time.

Why don't apologies work? I know I've said a few bad jokes, and it seems everyone takes it so personally.

As humbling as her phone calls were, the unfortunate event haunted the convention for years to come.

"Hey, Sally. You're going to invite Chippendales next year to perform?"

Apologies were accepted, but the event itself remained irreparable and unforgettable. It will always live in the land of legends, and is a reminder to all of us, scope your material out first. If it's in your head—ask yourself would my sister/brother/grandmother/grandfather/mother/father find this acceptable? If you plan to present the humor to the entire staff, listen to it first before it's ever presented in public.

Though one would hope situations like this could repair themselves, jokes, phrases, actions, cartoons, and one-liners haunt people's reputations. What we often remember is not the complimentary enriched statements told to us by fellow employees and employers. What sticks in our memories is most often outrageous moments: the condescending remarks, the exposed breast at the Super Bowl, the cell phone call interrupting a speech at the NRA convention, or a vulgar reference to an all-woman's basketball team on a national radio program. In our more self-contained environment at work, we may not be as exposed to public scrutiny, but our remarks are still heard, remembered, and judged. "You are more quotable than you think." And as easy as it may be to trip and say the wrong thing, it can be just as easily controlled by considering a few important action steps.

Action Steps

1. Your words are important. Keep track of every one of them.

2. If you are a joke teller, do it on stage with your friends. Don't tell them at work. After all, the jokes you tell are a reflection of who you are.

3. Avoid letting the stupid switch take over. Never assume. Look into material first before it is presented at work. Develop a healthy sense of doubt.

4. Become a person of class. Be a good role model. Great professionalism that we see in great leaders often leads to financial, emotional, and professional success.

5. No jokes are truly private at work. Refrain from sharing any kind of humor that could be heard, seen, re-counted, or re-sorted by someone at work. You don't want your own humor to haunt you.

6. Be a change agent, says Shoshana Brower, diversity expert. "Speak up if someone makes offensive jokes or comments. Remember what you permit, you promote. If you don't step up to the plate publicly or privately and let others know that their humor is offensive, then, in essence, you become part of the problem."

And now I have a question for you...

Many of us tell jokes without realizing they're offensive. We're simply blind to the effect it has on others. When I asked a comedy writer about a recent incident on *Desperate Housewives* denigrating doctors from the Philippines, she said the joke went right past her. "I either didn't hear it or it simply didn't bother me, but had I been Filipino, it would have been a different story. I too would have felt offended, and had I been a writer on the show, I'd have eliminated that joke in a heart beat."

Do you need to be Fillipino to feel insulted? How do we increase our sensitivity so that we don't make these mistakes? What have you done in the workplace to create a safe environment and train people to be watchful of the words they use?

Chapter Ten

Road Rage on the Computer

How to Create Engaging E-mails That Get a Response, Not a Reaction.

> *When it comes to angry e-mails, ask yourself the following before hitting the Send key: Would you deliver the same message, in the same words, if you were within punching distance?*
>
> —*From* Send
>
> *Here's the tricky part. Our motives usually change without any conscious thought on our parts. When adrenaline does our thinking for us, our motives flow with the chemical tide.*
>
> —*Kerry Patterson*

One of the most violent, disagreeable, annoying e-mails Jane received at her new consulting job came from Bill, a colleague. It simply read:

Can't do it.

Bill.

Out of context this may not sound like a disaster, but Bill had asked Jane a favor. Would she take over an account with a particularly difficult customer? It would mean a lot to him and could prove lucrative for her. "You're a lot more tactful than I am, and I think you'll work fine with Marion. I'll meet with you ahead of time over coffee one morning and prep you before your first client meeting."

Jane reluctantly agreed, but she grew frustrated when Bill kept putting off their pre-client coffee chat. She dashed off an e-mail that said, "Bill, let's meet before my appointment tomorrow. I could use your support! Thanks, Jane."

And he replied with the infamous "Can't do it."

How am I going to do a good job if I don't get coaching ahead of time, as he promised? Jane thought. She felt powerless, having volunteered for something she didn't want to do. As a new employee, she felt she could show her team spirit by agreeing to take on this task, but now she felt suckered.

"Every time I volunteer for things like this, I get burned. I'm too nice," she told her husband that night. "I feel dumped on and ignored. Now I'm meeting a difficult customer tomorrow, and I'm hanging in the wind. I wonder if Bill did this on purpose to sabotage me."

"Call him at home," her husband insisted.

"I think he's in Chicago."

"He probably has his cell phone with him. Call him directly. Deal with it straight on. At the very least, find out what happened, Jane. Don't jump to conclusions."

Instead, Jane dashed off another e-mail to Bill:

From:	Jane
To:	Bill
cc:	
Subject:	Meeting with Ms. Peterson

Bill, you realize. I've never worked with Ms. Peterson before. You're the one that passed her on to me after you screwed up, and I don't appreciate you washing your hands of this matter. Why hand her to me if you're not going to take the time to prepare me with some research? If I blow it, it will make you, and I, and the company look bad. I need to talk with you, as you promised. When's a good time? My meeting is scheduled for noon tomorrow."

Jane

Bill's answer: *"How about the tenth of never?"*

Jane's answer: *"How about keeping your promise, scum bag."*

Bill: *"Whiner."*

E-mail writers? Ready to your battle stations. On your mark. Get set. Go!

If we wanted to play road rage, rent the game:

E-MAIL ROAD RAGE AVAILABLE ON PLAYSTATION III
Job wrecking at its best!
Don't miss one exciting moment of shame and humiliation!
It's more than just a game. It's unemployment!

If you want to resolve a conflict quickly, nothing beats a "live" conversation. Had Jane called Bill on his cell phone she could have asked questions, resolved issues right away, and hopefully moved toward a commitment. Because she chose to write the message while feeling angry and frustrated, she not only went with the "chemical tide" and let her emotions take over, but by putting it in writing she created a permanent imprint that—who knows?—could some day be used against her.

Michael Eisner, former president of Disney, once called e-mail the most important technological advance of the 20th century, and he also said: "It can make or break a reputation in seconds." Though e-mail has revolutionized our ability to communicate with almost anyone via the internet, an improperly written e-mail can land you in big trouble.

Cannonball E-mails

We write within the context of those who speak to us, and a sentence is basically just a bunch of words: nouns, verbs, adjectives, and the five other parts of speech, arranged syntactically.

"Can't do it."

Can't—this contraction may sound softer than "cannot," but when isolated, it sounds heartless.

Add "I," and the pronoun warms it up slightly. "I can't do it" sounds a bit more humane.

"I can't do it because...." sounds better. Add a reason, and you soften the message and tell the reader what's in it for her.

"Obviously, I can't do it" cools it down and adds that one little adverb that says, *You are an idiot!*

Within the context of a dialogue or chat, these three short words, "Can't do it," might have worked just fine. In fact, many times we appreciate even one-word responses. We understand the situation. All we need is a quick answer. On the other hand, not everyone will appreciate the brevity. Isolated, sent without any explanation or companion e-mail, placed on a lonely space across a 19-inch monitor, the word(s) "Can't do it" sound inflammatory, not succinct.

Ever get an e-mail that just says "Thanks"?

Set off by itself, "thanks" may be construed as insincere and cold indifference.

The easiest way to avoid this problem is to always include some level of sincere appreciation:

Hi, Jane. Sorry I didn't get back to you, but call me tonight. No worries.

Bill.

How difficult is that?

Why do people write these short canon-ball e-mails?

- ➤ They think faster is better. They believe they don't have the time to say anything else.
- ➤ They're either using their Blackberry or texting on a phone, so they abbreviate their thoughts.
- ➤ They purposely want to seek revenge.

Going-Nuclear E-mails

Jane's response to Bill blasted across the Internet universe, destroying everything in its path. Though we can assume highly aggressive people are prone to write these e-mails, they aren't the only ones. Even warm, friendly, outgoing listeners (the Relaters) will hold feelings in for a period of time and then *blast off!* Jane fears confrontation and would normally never approach someone "live" with such outraged emotions. That's why she rejects her husband's suggestion to call Bill. *Hey, I don't want to deal with him on the phone. I'll just send him an e-mail.*

Afraid to confront Bill on the phone, she feels no qualms about speaking her mind in writing, committing what is sometimes called "disinhibition." This is the act of letting our fingers do all the talking, pouring out emotions we would normally "inhibit" or hold back. Calvin Trilling calls them "vomit e-mails." We just let ourselves go on in ways we would never do if we were talking live with someone.

My suggestion: Use your "fail safe" button. Don't fill in the address of the person to whom you're writing until you've read your e-mail and let it sit. Draft it so it's saved. Always ask yourself each time you write an e-mail, "Should I put this in writing?" Consider getting rid of certain trigger phrases, comments, and sarcastic remarks, such as:

➢ Obviously
➢ In the first place
➢ Need
➢ Should
➢ Can't

Get rid of them! Develop a healthy sense of doubt. In other words, never send an e-mail without giving it some breathing room. *If I were* xyz, *would I appreciate what I just wrote here?*

Here's a little piece of the puzzle Bill didn't share with Jane: *He passed the client to Jane because Bill is being promoted and the move inundated him with work.*

Who's the culprit behind this communication glitch? We can blame Bill for his arrogance, but what responsibility does

181

Jane have for discovering the full picture? "Bill, tell me honestly why you want me to do this. What's going on? I can't volunteer unless I have the full picture." Had she probed, would the same e-mail war have erupted?

Devil's Advocate: Hold on! Hold on one bloody moment! Are you saying it's Jane's fault she didn't mindread this guy and find out what was really going on? I mean, are we in the detective business here?

Dr. Gary: Those of us who tend to shy away from confrontation tend to trust people and assume they always have good intentions. The problem with this philosophy is not just the naivety behind it, it's the lack of responsibility.

When you write an e-mail, it lasts forever. It can appear on CNN! Never put anything in writing that can be held against you. *It can be passed around the office. It can be printed in the newspaper! Never! (Forgive me. I'm repeating myself.) That's why you do your research first, have a live conversation, or find another means of communicating your message, other than in writing.*

10 Tips to Help You Create Engaging E-mails

When the adrenaline is flowing and if a live conversation is impossible, how do we express ourselves in writing to get our message across and achieve the outcome we want every time?

The wondrous aspects of e-mail abound. We can write to someone at any time, in any place. If we want to reply to a situation at 4 a.m., we can do so without fear of disturbing someone's sleep. And we can write to anyone in any location at any time, for not even the price of a stamp.

How good is that?

We can, however, fall into a number of traps. Here are 10 tips to help you shape your writing so even difficult messages will achieve the outcome you desire.

Tip #1: Be aware of the company e-mail policy.

An employee at a large company in a mythical city somewhere near Los Angeles, California, sent her boyfriend an e-mail describing what she was going to do to him that night. It was their anniversary. She pressed the send button so quickly she didn't realize she had mistakenly pressed "reply to all." Her pornographic love note was delivered to 85,000 employees world wide. Though the company fired her (the policy clearly stated "No personal e-mail"), she sued for her job back and won.

You know why?

At her pre-trial settlement meeting with the judge, she stated that if she were being fired for doing an "*oops*," then no problem. She'd leave. Case closed. But the company specifically fired her because she violated a policy no one followed. In fact, everyone on her team across the entire country, as far as she knew, wrote personal e-mails and visited personal Websites, despite the company's efforts to curb that habit.

How can you fire someone for violating a policy no one follows? So, given the enormity of the problem—all across America workers write personal e-mails—every company should create an enforceable e-mail policy that has some teeth to it.

Tip #2: While you're at it: Create your own personal e-mail policy.

By now you know the litany: Never send anything you wouldn't want others at your company to read. Psychologically, the impulsive, spontaneous person simply refuses to follow this advice. A few years ago, however, I started reading my e-mails after I sent them, and I was shocked at the amount of emotion (as well the plethora of errors) I didn't catch the first time. Now, if I believe the e-mail has even the slightest chance of haunting me, I read it 10 or 15 minutes later and then decide whether or not to send it.

Tip #3: Plan and organize your thoughts before you type the e-mail.

Seldom *ever* do I hear people outwardly compliment the writers of e-mails. "Oh, wow! I get the best e-mails. I understand everything that's said."

"No, everyone's so friendly and outgoing…it's just a pleasure. I can't wait to read my 275 e-mails every day!"

Will that ever happen?

"E-mail is perhaps the most contextually sensitive piece of writing we have and ultimately we're going through this stage where we don't understand how to read it."
—Sarah Myers McGinty

Some quick ways to organize your thoughts: Ask yourself what's your core message? A good way to determine core messages is to take a moment and brainstorm. Ask yourself the six journalism questions: who/what/where/why/when/how. Then, jot down your ideas. Generally your answers to the "what" and the "why" will constitute a good core message.

1. What do I want to say and why do I want to say it?
2. What do I want my reader to do?
3. What does the reader need to know from me to get this done?
4. What information should go inside this e-mail and what should I leave out?

In *Make it Stick*, the Heath brothers point out the importance of creating messages that are memorable and that stick. The first sentence in the e-mail is usually the most important. That's your core message, and sometimes it's worth the trouble crafting it.

Tip #4: Create an easy-to-find core message (Don't put your readers on a hunt).

Highly motivated readers will pore over an e-mail, even if it takes them awhile to search for the solution or main idea. In certain professions, we write and read e-mails that are complicated, hard to follow, and nonsensical, and we read them anyway because we love our jobs and we're...well...compulsive. *(What if I miss something?)*

Do you have staff members who aren't highly motivated, that don't love their jobs, and aren't detail oriented? If, for example, you're writing to a client, burying the message amidst loads of detail can be dangerous.

Here's an annoying little e-mail from text support I received recently. (I took out some of the software terms to protect the guilty.)

"The problem was found to be that the shshsht launches using Web start which in most configurations will take the proxy setting from the local machine. The proxy server configured in IE FL in this case would not forward traffic for port 8443. The solution is to override the proxy settings for the SPM host."

I have no idea what a proxy setting is, but as a consumer, I might have had a better chance of following these procedures had the writer simply put the solution up front:

"Override the proxy settings for the SPM host by..."

Then tell me what to do, step by step. Don't waste my time with all the irrelevant details. Try the MADE formula:

Make it easy for the reader by putting the **Message** up front.

Action Statement tells the reader what you want.

Details include any details you feel are important. If the reader is not interested in these details, they'll skip over them.

Evidence usually refers to attachments that you "attach" to the e-mail.

(Note: Some great examples and information on this MADE formula in Diana Booher's book *E -Writing*.)

If readers have to hunt for the message, they will give up. Only the most highly motivated, compliant readers will pore over a complicated, drawn out piece of writing. That's why procedures should be written at the simplest level. The more complicated the writing, the more "motivated" the reader has to be to get through it.

For example, if I am an attorney trying to sort out the details that formed the lawsuit *Smith Associates v. Sherry*, I'll want to see every detail and will expect that information in the e-mail itself, or in the **evidence**.

However, if I'm reading hundreds of e-mails and this involves a decision for installing my software, don't waste my time with all the details.

To: Gary Seigel

From: Anthem Text Support

Thank for you for your recent inquiry regarding installation. Try overriding the proxy settings. Here's how you do it: **Message/Action)**

1. Hold down the shift control and cap key all at once.
2. Press F10 key.
3. Computer will ask if you want to re-start. Say yes. Re-start.

The problem was found to be that the shshsht launches using Web start which in most configurations will take the proxy setting from the local machine. The proxy server configured in IE FL in this case would not forward traffic for port 8443. But by overriding the proxy setting, you should be just fine. **(Details)**

If you want to include details at the end, that's fine. I, personally, could care less, and I am not going to read them, but tech people may appreciate having that information. You can also put those details in an attachment so they don't clutter the core message.

Here's a rewrite of Bill's e-mail, after he decides to take the time and explain his situation.

Wrong version (not using MADE):

Jane,

I know we had talked about having me meet with you for a chat regarding Ms. Pedersen, but unfortunately, I'm stuck here in Chicago, and I have so many things going on. You wouldn't believe what I've been through. Though I accepted a new position, I had no idea I'd be doing the cleanup work for so many others, and on top of everything the transmission went out on my rental car, right on the toll road.

If you want to meet or talk via phone I can give you some background on Pedersen.

Would this evening be good for you, or let me know what's a good time?

Bill

Better version using the MADE formula:

I apologize for not setting a time to meet with you to go over the Pedersen account. I'm stuck here in Chicago, but I can speak to you tonight at 7p.m. (Pacific Time). Will that work?

Which one do you like better?

Write to express not to impress. Keep e-mails short. Use reasons, but choose them wisely.

Here's one more version—a bit longer:

Jane,

I apologize for making a promise I didn't keep. I am swamped, but in the meantime, this may help you. Here's what I know:

> ➤ *Client needs installation in every office (56 offices)*
> ➤ *Client did use Reynolds and Company and was dissatisfied. I don't know why.*
> ➤ *Client claims she saw our Website. No other references.*

If you want more, call me tonight. 800-585-8685 after 8 p.m. central time.

I will be glad to help you.

Bill

Tip #5: Learn proper grammar.

Some wonderful easy-to-read grammar books will solve this problem, but I have a couple of secrets that seem to work if you forget the rules. Don't tell anyone. Please don't share this with my fourth grade English teacher; she'll roll right out of heaven and hit me with a pitchfork.

If you're not sure how a word is spelled, whether it's capitalized or even what the proper syntax is—stick the phrase in a word engine like Google and see how other Websites use it. Now you might get it wrong—not all Websites get it right—but I found you'll see a pattern of phrases such as "eastern Arkansas" capitalized? (No). Is "someone" singular or plural? (Singular) Is it "between you and me" or "between you and I"? (between you and me). Yes, I can recommend you learn the rules, but at least you have at your fingertips a way to see how other "experts" solve your particular grammatical or spelling problem. And by the way, grammar check doesn't work well, so when in doubt, leave it out, or look up the rule in a good style guide.

Tip #6: Proofread!

At almost every level of the American work force, people who write via e-mail, blogs, and texting have a multitude of challenges—one of which is THE STUPID ERROR.

It's form you, isn't it?

I thought it was they're responsibility.

Its not going happen.

All of above have errors, as does this sentence.

Why do we make errors like this and why can't we see them?

Apparently, we think in terms of narrative. So if you write a sentence such as the one below...

"The circle performers walked the elephant down Main Street."

...the brain's thinking "circus performers" even though your fingers typed "circle." You, the reader, might see "circle" very clearly, but the person who wrote this sentence—who lived this narrative in his head—may not be able to see it. He's thinking "circus," but he writes "circle." If he reads it aloud, he may catch the error. If he prints it on colored paper or enlarges the font on the screen, that may help as well.

In other words, trick the brain into finding the error by making your text appear like something the brain has never seen before. Printing it on pink paper, for example, would do that. When we misspell names or call a female "Mr." or put the plaintiff's name in a space where the defendant's name belongs, these "stupid" errors ultimately decrease our credibility. We can catch these errors by becoming compliant and analytical. Move yourself into the Thinker/Analyzer mode we discussed in the Chapter 4, and focus on every word...every letter...every sentence. Develop a healthy sense of doubt.

1. Print it on colored paper so the brain says, "Wow, what's that?"
2. Read it aloud.
3. Take a break.
4. Read it backwards, sentence by sentence.
5. Have someone else read it to you.

Never print your final copy until you've allowed the brain to see the document with fresh eyes.

Now a moment of truth. Decades ago, while I was teaching (for eight weeks) at a high school, I had a book review printed in the *LA Times*. A couple of weeks after it came out, a little editorial blurb in the *LA Times* read, "High School English Teacher Destroys English Language." I thought—wow the poor guy. He must be so embarrassed. How awful for him! Of course, I soon discovered the poor guy was me. I had misspelled the word "pore." You "pore" over a manuscript. You don't "pour" over it. And because I made that glaring error, the "reader" pored over my writing and found other minor errors.

By the way, do you think I ever misspelled that word "pore" again?

Ever since then, I proofread my writing and ask for help. Finding a colleague or friend to proofread your work isn't a bad idea.

Tip #7: Customize the message to your reader.

When reading e-mails, you can often "read" the person's personality based on the sentences. A short, direct e-mail with bullet points suggests you're dealing with a director who wants the bottom line. If you read an e-mail filled with details or step by step instructions, the reader may be more "indirect."

A more "closed approach" sticks to the facts and leaves out personal information. A more "open approach" includes warmth and emotion.

Here's an example.

You have an amazing lunch with a potential boss. Afterward, you send this e-mail:

Wow! What a wonderful lunch! Thank you so much. I enjoyed hearing about your trip to Peru, and I look forward to speaking to you again. Here's the information you requested. I'm available for an interview any time next week, and by then you can call my office for a referral. Hope your son gets into MIT!

Best regards,

Sally

(Personally, this warms my heart. Some people would gag on all the warmth. Here's a more direct alternative.)

Thanks for a great lunch. Here's the information you requested. I look forward to hearing from you.

Sally.

Notice there's no excitement about the job and no mention of her interest in working for this company, but it sticks to the point and avoids sidetracking personal information that "closed" or "self-contained" people don't want to read.

A direct approach (probably the way to go in most e-mails) is to state the main idea up front and keep it short.

An indirect approach includes many details (possibly an attachment), and may cover the subject from several angles.

Tip #8: If you deliver bad news, send it quickly.

Try not to put bad news in an e-mail. Call a person on the phone or have a live conversation. If you have to send bad news, Shipley and Schwalbe in *Send* suggest sending it quickly. In other words, just say it. Don't add a lot of qualifiers.

"I can't make the meeting this Friday, but please fill me in with the details on Monday so that I can help you finish the project."

versus

"I wish I could make the meeting. I have so much going on, but you can count on me next time, rest assured."

(How do you know that? Maybe you'll be out of town. Maybe you truly don't care! The second one might come off as a lie so be careful.)

Don't put anything in writing you're not absolutely certain you can do.

So what do you do when you have bad news?

Just say it.

Even this statement, "This is not something I can do right now," suggests that in the future you might be able to do it. Don't soften it unless you mean that.

Just say the bad news. Here's an easy formula:

Buffer it, Break it to 'em, Befriend them.

Your first sentence buffers it.

"Thanks for inviting me."

The second sentence states your message.

"I'm out of town, and I can't make the meeting."

And the third sentence ends with rapport.

"I'll look forward to hearing how it went. Gary."

Here is a sample of bad news:

Wrong Way:

"Sorry we're out of the CD you requested. It should come out in August. Let us know if you want us to send it to you as soon as it arrives. Thanks."

Alternative Way:

"Thank you for purchasing the new CD Sinatra and Elvis: the Duets *from Merck Publishers. This new recording has received rave views from* Publishing Weekly *and* CD Today *and we think you will love it.*

"The print date changed to August 2008, and we will have it shipped to you as soon it arrives. As a special gift (we apologize for the long wait), we are including a preview CD of Sinatra and Dylan: the Duets—*unavailable to the public and just for your review."*

Tip #9: Don't waste the reader's time.
Put the subject in the subject line.

"I can't make the meeting." vs. "meeting."

"Tuesday's 7 a.m. meeting on benefit plan" vs. "benefit plan meeting"

"7 a.m. Krispy Kremes 7:05 gone" vs. "Be on time."

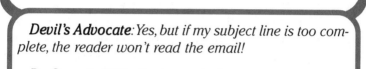

Devil's Advocate: Yes, but if my subject line is too complete, the reader won't read the email!

Dr. Gary: So? What's your point?

Tip #10: QTIP

When I made a grammar error in one of my first articles many decades ago, I went on a rampage and blamed the editor of the *LA Times*.

"Why didn't you catch those errors?" I yelled.

He laughed and threw a QTIP at me. He said, "Seigel, quit taking it personally(QTIP)."

In other words, he was one of many who suggested I take full responsibility for my writing and learn to do it right.

In my writing workshops, I always ask the groups if they like to write. Few hands go up. Part of the reason for this, I think, is that we live in fear that we'll embarrass ourselves or people won't appreciate what we say in writing. Either we had unpleasant experiences in school (our teachers red-inked our papers to death) or we feel frustrated by the writing process. *It takes too long! It's too hard! I'm not good at it!*

If you share these frustrations, know you're in good company. Though most of us communicate via e-mail, a massive majority of e-mail writers *hate* to write.

Take time to practice. Check some of the resources at the back of the book and on the Website or enroll in a writing class that will hopefully diffuse the fear and make you realize—we all make mistakes, and we all have the ability to correct them.

Now I have a question for you...

How would you rewrite this e-mail to eradicate any hint of road rage and make the core message clear?

John Smith called this morning and said that he couldn't be here until the end of the week to show the samples of the new chairs and desks that we need for the conference on Tuesday. I told him that this was the fourth time that his office had canceled or postponed an appointment. And I was a bit rude because I am tired of dealing with these people. If you ask me, their office products are no better than what we used in the other office, and I'm sure their price is going to be higher although John insists that with volume discounts we can save a bundle though he wouldn't tell me what the bundle was (big mystery! I guess! I can't wait for the surprise!) Do you have some overwhelming reason to continue to deal with these people or can I call the original vendor we used at our previous location and make the order. Let me know because I'd like to get these tables and chairs ordered quickly before the conference.

—Phyllis.

Chapter Eleven

How to Recover After You Put Your Foot in Your Mouth

The Art of Making Apologies

Remember our relationships are our keys to ourselves. How we treat others is how we will ultimately want to be treated.

—*Greesh C. Sharman*

Devil's Advocate*: Before you get started here, let me say that all the famous people who have recently apologized for drunken comments, racial slurs, moral misconduct, and tirades* never *seem to get it right. It doesn't matter what they say, they're criticized for it. That makes me think I should just keep my mouth shut and not even bother apologizing.*

> *Dr. Gary: No question—we witness many bad apologies. It's difficult for famous people to admit doing wrong, especially if the humiliating facts will impact their careers. They either divulge too much, or they're so guarded that they don't say enough. When we put a foot in our mouths during a business encounter, we may want to ask: What will it take for me to clean up my mistake and minimize the consequences? This chapter explores key strategies for damage control.*

Bad Apologies

Supervisor: *"Manny?"*

Employee: *"Yes."*

S: "Did you just hang up on that customer?"

E: "No."

S: "I overheard the conversation. You swore and slammed the phone down."

E: "No I didn't. I was just finishing a conversation."

S: "Manny, I was standing outside the hall. I was just about to knock and come in to talk to you."

E: "You were spying on me?"

S: "That's not what I said. I heard you speak. Walls are thin. And you sounded like a mad dog."

E: "You know what? I'm really tired of your petty criticism and micromanaging. You don't know the situation. I handled it the best I could. And I'd appreciate it if you would get out of my office and mind your own frickin' business, and stop being Mr. CIA. Okay?"

An hour later, the boss calls Manny into his office, accuses him of lying, speaking abusively to a customer and a fellow employee, and mishandling a situation that could cost the company an important account. The boss tells Manny, "I'll take care of the customer. I know she's very difficult, but George is your manager, and he's ready to let you go. I suggest you apologize quickly before he does something you'll regret."

Manny shook his head. "I don't appreciate being spied on. Maybe I could have handled the customer more tactfully, but I did the best I could under the circumstances."

"I don't know if you heard what I said," the boss replied. "Go clean up your act. Speak with George."

Apologizing for a mistake can be challenging. We may not work in the most forgiving environment, and what we say—whether purposely or by accident—may be so hurtful that the recovery process simply takes a long time. Apologizing correctly is an art, and the most important factor is facing the issue.

Apology Attempt #1

"George, you have to understand that sometimes you act like a hovercraft. You're just hovering over people all the time, and that drives me crazy. If you'll stop doing that, I'm sure in the future you won't get such a reaction from me." *(I give this one an F)*

Blaming the situation on someone else hardly qualifies as an appropriate apology.

Apology Attempt #2

"George, I'm sorry if I hurt you. I have a lot on my mind. You just came in at the wrong time. Okay?" *(Perhaps deserving of a C-)*

This one isn't much better, because Manny blames George's timing. Though he did say "I'm sorry," the subtext is: *If you'd come in later, I wouldn't have acted this way.*

Both these apologies are ineffective because they sidestep the real issue. Here are suggestions from a variety of experts who want to help us gracefully remove those feet from our mouths. We'll also look at some better versions of Manny's apology.

Admit to a Stupid Mistake

Admit to a stupid mistake. "I lost it. I apologize. I mishandled that customer and I spoke defensively and cruelly to you. Please forgive me." In his book, *I Can't Believe I Just Did That*, David Allyn says, "The more honest we are, the more proud of ourselves we become. That pride leads to confidence, which almost inevitably leads to achievement."

Speak up and speak out.

So often we apologize half-heartedly, and that lukewarm apology will haunt us later.

Ever apologize and the person just stares back at you, indifferently?

Even hours later, you're getting the cold shoulder and a couple of door slams.

Finally, you stand in the middle of the room, and say: "For crying out loud! I don't know why you're upset. I apologized. What more do you want?"

There's more.

Take Full Responsibility

This is a braver approach and makes the apology complete, but it can also open up a new can of worms. How much do I say? Is it worth taking a risk and putting all my cards on the table? Will it haunt me for the rest of my career? If Manny says nothing or if he waits too long, George could be building a case against him: *You're are a lying son of a bitch, and I'm going to fire your ass.* The sooner Manny changes that thought, the better.

How does he do that?

Embedded in the previous bad apologies is the admission from Manny that he erred, but if he were to take full responsibility, he'd cover all three of the errors he committed:

1. He lied.

2. He mistreated a customer.

3. He was rude and abusive to George.

If Manny leaves out one of those issues, it may come back to haunt him sooner or later. Facing all the issues won't make them go away, but they'll be acknowledged, recognized, and hopefully repaired. If he waits too long to apologize, add one more to the list.

4. He waited too long to apologize.

Apologies Work Best When They Rely on "I" Statements

Once we understand the problem, invest in the outcome, plan to match our body language to the message, and find the most appropriate time and place to deliver the apology, it's time to actually speak the words. And those words should be "I" statements.

Manny's script might sound like this, a variation of some of the suggestions we saw earlier:

Manny: George, I want to apologize. I didn't handle that customer right and you were correct in pointing that out to me. I'm sorry I got defensive and took it out on you. Next time I have an angry customer, I'll put her on hold and get control of my emotions before I speak. Also, I should never have taken it out on you; that was very wrong of me.

When a person not only recognizes the mistake, but makes a commitment to change, the apology becomes more powerful and sincere. If Manny does indeed work on his behavior and consciously avoids making the same mistakes again, he might eventually say to George. "You know for the past month or so, I've really been working on my temper and communicating more effectively with the customers. How am I doing?"

Sometimes You Just Have to Clean Up Your Act: The Case of the Rude Rental Car Agent

In Chapter 1, I included an exercise in which Phil, a rental car agent, rudely dismissed a customer's request to exchange a rental car that smelled of cigarette smoke for one that was smoke free.

"All our cars are non-smoking cars, Mack," Phil told his customer.

Instead of listening and calmly trying to resolve the customer's complaint, Phil kept returning to his phone call with his angry ex-wife and, at one point, snapped at the customer in an attempt to get rid of him.

Fortunately for Phil, the customer was very patient. While Phil spoke on the phone to the ex wife, the customer slid his business card across the counter. It said: *Reynaldo Hernandez, Ph.D.* and listed his profession as **communication specialist**.

"What are you? A therapist?" the agent asked, staring at the card.

Dr. Hernandez nodded.

The agent shook his head, pointed to the phone and covered the mouth piece with the palm of his hand. Then he turned to the customer and said, "THIS WOMAN IS DRIVING ME NUTS!"

"I feel your pain," Dr. Hernandez replied. "How did this all get started? Talk to me. What was your childhood like?"

Phil laughed. It was 1 a.m. in the morning. His ex wife was violating a child custody ruling, and this customer wanted to dish out therapy. Realizing Dr. Hernandez was just trying to make him feel better, Phil apologized.

"I'm really sorry. I'm going through a crisis here."

"That's okay. I just want a non-smoking car," Dr. Hernandez replied.

Realizing he only had luxury cars available, Phil figured if he upgraded the customer, he'd have the guy out of his office, and he could return to his heated discussion with Alice. It would also be a nice thing to do considering how rude he had been.

Five minutes later, the customer drove off inside a Mercedes equipped with Satellite Radio, GPS system, leather seats, and On Star, and Phil returned to his phone call with Alice.

What Phil didn't realize was that all the other rental car company agents in the Seattle airport could hear the entire conversation. After all, the rental agencies share common walls—no front wall. Not only did they hear the way he spoke to the customer, but they heard nearly an hour of Phil volleying insults to his wife. Only when Phil's shift ended (7 a.m.) did it dawn on him that his competitors probably heard his marital woes and witnessed his poor customer service skills.

Would they keep their big mouths shut?

Instead of calling his manager right away and preventing what might have been a pipeline of gossip from the mouths of competitors to supervisors to Phil's manager—Phil went home to his apartment and fell asleep. When he awoke later that afternoon, he had an urgent voice mail message from not just the manager of the local branch—but the head of customer service in Chicago.

"Call me immediately."

Phil listened to the man's message but only half-heartedly—he heard phrases like "inappropriate conduct," "using phone for personal time," and "completely unaccept-able customer service skills" bouncing off the man's lips like bullets, and Phil had the sinking feeling that he would be fired.

He was right.

Had Phil fielded the potential criticism right at 7 a.m., the results may have been different. He could have used what David Allyn calls "fact defrosting." Confess the crime. "Listen there's something I need to clean up. I made a terrible mis-take. I am going through a horrible child-custody battle, and I used up company time. I took it out on my customer, and I am embarrassed and angry at myself. I don't think the customer will complain because I took care of him, but I wanted to let you know in case some of the other rental car agents say something. I'm just horribly embarrassed. What would you suggest I do?"

He may still lose his job, but by "fact defrosting," Phil avoids this other issue that often gets us in trouble—"Why did you wait so long to tell me? Why did I have to hear about this from our competitors? "

Placing our cards on the table—cleaning up our act—can be challenging and yet it can often save our reputations as well as our jobs. To have our mistakes unearthed makes us seem like we're hiding something. To disclose and be honest about it is—in many ways—an act of great courage.

As You Apologize, Listen to the Other Person

In this story, based on a real incident, Phil redeemed himself.

He used his own money, flew to Chicago, and waited a full day to meet with the president of the company, who prom-ised the Seattle agent five minutes of his time.

Late in the day, the secretary ushered Phil into the president's office.

"I've only come to listen," Phil told him. "You already know what I did, and I will never do that again, because I want to learn from this error, so history doesn't repeat itself. You're a very successful man, and I've admired you for years. What could I have done differently?"

Here's the key to Phil's amazing recovery. He developed a sincere need to fully understand the enormity of his mistake and the repercussions one bad night could have on a company's reputation.

He didn't dismiss it. ("You know I'm going through a lot. If you only knew.") He didn't blame it on anyone else. He didn't discount the crime. ("I don't know what the big deal is. I gave the customer what he wanted. He left happy!") And he didn't use the often overused excuse. ("So who hasn't used company time to solve personal problems? My gosh, it was 2 a.m.!") Most importantly, he didn't discredit the job. ("It was a lousy loser job anyway.") He took full responsibility. When the president of the company asked Phil what he believed he did wrong, Phil listed four aspects of the nightmare:

1. The customer service issue
2. The loss of productivity
3. The image the company has in the eyes of the customer and the other vendors
4. Taking company time to deal with personal issues.

Did he lose his job? Yes.

Did the president acknowledge and appreciate Phil's attempt to understand the issues? Absolutely, and after some encouraging advice, a few months of therapy, and a Tony Robbins workshop, Phil found a job he loved, with decent hours and a short commute from his home.

(Don't you love happy endings?)

The president also wrote him a letter of recommendation.

At the very least—even if we find it too challenging to reveal everything we did wrong—apologies often depend on extremely careful listening so that we hear all the complaints and can address them, one by one.

Often, however, we don't identify the real problem because we aren't listening. Here's an example of that:

The Case of the Ice-Cream Eating Secretary

Ellen: I felt embarrassed by the way you treated me in front of the team at our luncheon today.

Jack: I'm sorry. All I said was I worried about the amount of sugar you eat.

Ellen: No, you said "Why don't you lay off the ice cream." You're my boss. You're not my doctor.

Jack: I was trying to help you avoid a diabetic attack. Excuse me for trying to save your life!

Ellen: I have my diabetes under control, thank you very much, and I was embarrassed that you brought this up with Tom and Sandy and the whole team sitting right there.

Jack: What am I supposed to do, just keep quiet? I can't afford to have you not here in the office tomorrow.

Ellen: What did I ask you to do?

Jack: I asked you to lay off the ice cream.

Ellen: No, what did I ask you to do?

Jack: Don't remind you that you could die if you eat the ice cream?

Ellen: Jack, you've been my boss for 20 years, and I can't believe you don't hear me.

Jack: I can't believe you. I bring up your health and you're throwing a fit.

Ellen: *Because you did it in front of Tom and Sandy and the whole group. That's why I'm livid.*

So many times, apologies don't work for us because the person apologizing doesn't hear the entire problem and therefore does not acknowledge it. Listen for subtext. Listen between the lines. Ask questions and probe so you fully understand *all* the issues. Ellen wants Jack to say, "I apologize for not taking you aside and speaking to you privately. That was stupid of me. But I rely on you. When you get sick and miss work, everyone suffers. I want your help: What should I do when I think you may be making a bad decision with food?" Ellen might respond, "Don't interfere. You're my boss, not my conscience. Let me make that decision by myself. If you insist on a discussion with me, at least do it in private."

Before You Apologize, Do Your Research

Here are a few embarrassing examples of what happens when we don't do our research.

From Manny's apology

Manny: I regret what I said. I really do, but Mrs. Lennox didn't know what she was talking about.

George: First of all her name is Sally Lexus...like the car...and she's a doctor. Dr. Lexus. A very smart woman.

From Phil's apology at 5 a.m. in the airport

Phil: Sorry guys. (Turns to the Sun Coast Car Rental Agency Representative) I guess I kind of made a fool out of myself tonight, but the customer seemed happy.

Other agent: Don't worry about it.

(He should worry about it. We can't always take what people say at face value.)

The Mouth Trap

From Jack's apology for embarrassing Ellen in front of the team

Jack: Ellen, I am so sorry I embarrassed you this afternoon at the meeting. I just didn't know what to do. Frankly, I wasn't sure you even knew what you were ordering.

Ellen: First of all, it wasn't ice cream. It was sugar-free non-dairy tofu, and I wasn't mad at you for that. I was furious you tried to humiliate me in front of the team!

Knowing your facts is especially important when diversity issues or off-color jokes surface

"I'm sorry I made that anti-Jewish remark." (You mean that anti-Semitic remark, right?)

"I don't know what the big deal is...I've always been a friend of the Afro-American community." (You mean African-American community)

"At the very least, let's let bygones be bygones, smoke the peace pipe, have a pow wow and end these disagreements." (I'm Native American and those phrases offend me.)

When we truly offend someone with remarks made against an ethnic group, this often suggests a much larger issue that can't be resolved by one conversation. At the very least, do your research. Use the right terminology. Ask questions. Plan your apology carefully.

"I'm so sorry if I offended you. I'm ignorant on this. What terms are appropriate to use?"

When you're dealing with belief systems, every word is important.

Respect and understand the issue thoroughly.

Learn about the issue and respect the listener's perspective.

Create the Visible Effect

Many times we simply aren't invested in the apology. We're thinking, *what's the big deal? Don't they have better things to do than complain about this? But, hey, it's my job, and I'll make it right.* The syntax of our words may suggest sincerity, but our body language betrays us. We shrug our shoulders, roll our eyes, or avoid eye contact. With a simple movement of our arms and hands, we can dismiss everything we've said.

This doesn't mean you have to "stage" an apology as some politicians do, standing behind a desk with pictures of the family and an American flag. Nevertheless, you want to show you're upset and sincere. Make certain you believe what you say and that your body (your face/movement/posture) backs you up.

Create Restitution/Reparations

If you take my pen and say you are sorry, but don't give me the pen back, nothing has happened.
—Bishop Desmond Tutu

So you say the wrong things repeatedly. You've been warned, but you don't change your behavior. This could spell trouble. Yet, what if you apologize and then change your behavior? You're more careful with words. You even enroll in a training program. If you do all that, the offending party is more likely to find the grace to forgive.

Manny, for example, is likely to repeat the behavior we saw earlier unless he makes a commitment to controlling his rage. Manny should ask himself: *What do I need to do to avoid these public confrontations so I don't humiliate myself and anger others?* Maybe he takes an anger management class or enrolls in group therapy. Whatever it may be, Manny's first task is to own the problem, take the responsibility to correct the behavior, and consistently monitor his results.

Phil made a concerted effort to uncover an issue that could destroy his career: He was allowing his personal life to infiltrate and sabotage his customer service skills, and he made a somewhat painful, public commitment to effect change. That's why he flew to Chicago, sat for eight hours waiting for an appointment, and shared his regret with the owner of the rental car agency. One would hope that the pain Phil suffered (loss of a job, eight hours sitting in an office, months off with no pay) would create such an impact on his life that it would forever remind him to focus on upgrading his customer service skills.

Tony Robbins says, "Once we effect a change, we should reinforce it immediately. Then, we have to condition our nervous systems to succeed not just once, but consistently."

Phil and Manny, for example, have to consistently practice their new skills, and they would probably have a greater chance of success if their improved skills were recognized. "Manny, you did a great job!" "Phil, I just want you to know that that was a difficult situation and you handled it beautifully!" Showing appreciation and recognizing improvement are two freebies any business professional can afford and the rewards are enormous. Employees feel safer. They gain a greater sense of self-worth, and they perceive true camaraderie and fellowship that encourages them to do and say the right thing on a consistent basis.

Of course, restitution can go too far. When we deliver too many thanks and too many presents, it comes off as "brown nosing" and "placating" and that's not going to get you the results you want.

When we've hurt someone, though, we can create restitution by writing a note, sending flowers, or performing some unexpected act of kindness like surprising someone with a free car wash or a Starbuck's gift card. More importantly, restitution and repair work becomes even more effective when the person who received the apology recognizes the changed behavior, and says something. For example, when Jane notices her boss taking her aside to speak to her privately, she shows appreciation and thanks him for his efforts. When a boss realizes his supervisor went to some lengths to issue an apology, it may only take a wink or a handshake or a silent nod of agreement, but sincere apologies will resonate and radiate longer and better if they are dutifully accepted and graciously acknowledged.

Action Steps for Making the Apology

1. Take responsibility for your action and delineate the issues.
2. Choose the right time to make your apology.
3. Repair the situation by offering to change your behavior or seek a solution.
4. Listen to the other person's explanation.
5. Speak clearly and concisely, using "I" statements.
6. Allow your body language to match the sincerity of your words.
7. Believe in the power of the thought behind the apology and the impact will be greater.

Action Steps for the Person Receiving an Apology

1. When receiving an apology, don't placate the person with "forget about it" or "It's no big deal." Deal directly with it. Be honest.

2. Once the apology has been offered, don't keep reminding the person of the mistake he or she made. Don't be a guilt-maker.

3. Stay on topic. Don't veer onto other issues that weren't resolved.

4. Embrace forgiveness.

5. Say "Thank you," and show appreciation.

And now I have a question for you...

You and a customer ,Marianne, meet at a restaurant. After lunch, Marianne agrees to follow you (in her own car) to your office. Unfortunately, you stop at a red light suddenly and she plows into you, severely damaging your car. Now your new car won't even run and a tow truck hauls it away. You're furious at Marianne, but you hold it in and treat her politely. She apologizes and promises to have her insurance company call you.

Later that day, a person who witnessed the accident calls and tells you Marianne was talking on the cell phone and seemed quite distracted. You realize you'll be out of a car for weeks, that Marianne had plenty of time to stop, and that had she not been blabbing on her cell phone, she would have paid attention to the red lights on your rear bumper. Furthermore, you will have to rent a car, deal with the time and expense of having your car fixed, and be stuck with a car forever tainted by a rear end collision. You're pissed off. You don't want to lose this customer, but you know your feelings will surface every time you have to deal with her.

What do you do? What kind of apology from Marianne would clean the slate?

Postscript

In the beginning of the book, I shared a story about a fictional prime minister whose poor communication skills and passive aggressiveness not only lost him his position in court but cost him his life. A poor role model, Pierre d'Pardoneau simply lacked the ability—the skill and the know-how—to achieve the outcome he desperately wanted.

At the same time, I dedicated The *Mouth Trap* to a more polished communicator and a real person—my father, David Seigel, an entrepreneur, a pioneer of television advertising, the author of five business books, and an inspiration not only to his four children but to thousands of business professionals who enrolled in his classes from 1973 to 1995.

My father's story, unlike Pierre's, ended happily. His engaging style won over even his severest critics. Had he lived several centuries earlier, he would have sniffed out a coup way before it happened and became fast friends with his darkest foes.

That's just the kind of guy he was. Like Will Rogers, it seems he never met a person he didn't like or appreciate.

The Mouth Trap

Though my father studied to be a lawyer and graduated from law school in Cleveland, Ohio, he chose instead to join his four brothers in Los Angeles to create Riviera Convertible Sofas, a company that eventually became a leader in home furnishings.

Legend has it that one Saturday night in the early 50s, millions of television viewers turned on their TV sets and no matter what local Los Angeles channel they viewed, they would only see one show: *The Art Linkletter Show* sponsored by Riviera. Unbeknownst to each local network, my father managed to buy all the advertising space, monopolizing that one hour. The company's slogan—"Live on the Riviera: Convertible Sofa, that is"—branded the company overnight.

And he did it without pissing anybody off.

Humorous, outgoing, personable, outspoken, assertive, but highly sociable, my dad closed deals based on wit, his intelligence, and engaging personality.

Like other great communicators, he valued the power of the word, and he measured his words and used each one wisely.

You often hear of entrepreneurs who toss their weight around. Many famous leaders have a reputation for being arrogant, autocratic, and difficult. Highly successful business professionals like Harvey Weinstein at Miramax, producer Scott Rudin, Martha Stewart, Donald Trump, and Michael Eisner develop a reputation for terse comments and tough mindedness. It's just the nature of the beast, some say, and who can argue with their success? It works for them and frankly, many of us wouldn't mind a little of their chutzpah.

But my dad taught me that not every successful business professional has to take on a ballistic style. You get people to do what you want by saying it the way they want it said. Because people spend a huge chunk of their lives in the workplace, he encouraged his students and children to create a comfortable environment. "For God's sake, if you create resistance, you'll start a war. Go in with a friendly attitude, show you care and appreciate the other person. Think Gandhi, not Attila the Hun."

Though he and his brothers sold Riviera in the late 1960s, David Seigel went on to become one of the most popular teachers at Pierce College in Woodland Hills, and so he passed his love for clear, engaging communication to thousands of aspiring entrepreneurs.

His belief that you can get what you want by speaking respectfully to others must have been engrained in him, for even as he suffered the throes of Alzheimer's for nearly 12 years, he never assumed any of the disagreeable behavior often associated with that disease. To the last days of his life, at age 87, he remained a "prince among men," an expression he often used to describe any listener who'd take the time to hear his stories.

Hopefully this book, influenced by his teachings and lessons, plus the dozens of writers and communication experts quoted in these chapters, will help you achieve the results you want both at home and at the office. But nothing happens unless we put it into practice.

Go onto the Website (*www.themouthtrap.com*) and share your experiences, your answers, and your suggestions. Then we can work together to create a community that respects and honors each other, producing outcomes we desire and relationships we want to sustain.

Bibliography

Alessandra,Tony and Phil Hunsaker. *Communicating at Work: Improve Your Speaking, Listening, Presentation, and Correspondence Skills To Get More Done and Get What You Want At Work.* New York: Fireside, 1993.

Allen, David. *Getting Things Done: The Art of Stress-Free Productivity.* New York: Penguin, 2003.

Allyn, David. *I Can't Believe I Just Did That: How Embarrassment Can Wreak Havoc in Your Life—and What You Can Do to Conquer It.* New York: MJF Books, 2004.

Booher, Dianna. *E-Writing. 21st Century Tools for Effective Communication.* New York: Pocket Books, 2001.

Carter-Scott, Sherie. *Negaholic: How to Overcome Negativity and Turn Your Life Around.* New York: Random House, 1999.

Covey, Stephen. *The Seven Habits of Highly Effective People.* New York: Free Press, 1989.

Crowley, Katherine and Kathi Elster. *Working with You is Killing Me: Freeing Yourself from Emotional Traps at Work.* New York: Time Warner, 2006.

Fournies, Ferdinand F. *Coaching for Improved Work Performance.* New York: McGraw Hill, 2000.

Gilliam, Joe. *The Winner in You: Be Your Own Hero.* Audio Recording. Kansas City: Rockhurst University Continuing Education Center, Inc., 2000.

Hartley, Gregory and Maryann Karinch. *How to Spot a Liar: Why People Don't Tell the Truth and How You Can Catch Them.* Franklin Lakes, NJ: Career Press, 2005.

Heath, Chip and Dan. *Make it Stick.* New York: Random House, 2007.

Hoover, John. *How to Work for an Idiot: Survive and Thrive Without Killing Your Boss.* Franklin Lakes, NJ: Career Press, 2004.

Jett Aal, Pamela. *Communicate With Confidence.* Audio Recording. Kansas City: Rockhurst University Continuing Education Center, Inc. 2005.

McGinty, Sarah Myers. *Power Talk.* New York: Warner Books, 2001.

Patterson, Kerry and Joseph Grenny, Ron McMillan, and Al Switzler. *Crucial Conversations: Tools for Talking When Stakes are High.* New York: McGraw Hill, 2002.

Pease, Alan and Barbara. *The Definitive Book of Body Language.* New York: Bantam Dell, 2004.

Robbins, Tony. *Awaken the Giant Within.* New York: Fireside, 1992.

Scott, Susan. *Fierce Conversations: Achieving Success at Work and in Life, One Conversation at a Time.* New York: Berkeley Publishing Group, 2002.

Shipley, David and Will Schwalbe. *Send: The Essential Guide to Email for Office and Home.* New York: Knopf, 2007.

Simmons, Annette. *Story Factor.* New York: Basic Books, 2001.

Stone, Douglas, Bruce Patton, and Sheila Heen. *Difficult Conversations: How to Discuss What Matters Most.* New York: Penguin Books, 1999.

Sutton, Robert. *The No Asshole Rule: Building a Civilized Workplace and Surviving One That Isn't.* New York: Warner Business Books, 2007.

Van Kerckhove, Carmen. Blog: *www.raceintheworkplace.com/2007/07/31/how-to-respond-to-a-racist-joke/*

Wagner, Bill. *The Entrepreneur Next Door: Discover the Secrets to Financial Independence.* New York: Entrepreneur Press, 2006.

Index

About the Author

Gary Seigel, Ph.D., is a trainer, writer, and motivational speaker. Based in Los Angeles, California. Dr. Gary inspires audiences nation-wide to write and speak with tact and finesse. His clients include Yahoo, Chevron, Symantec, the United States Navy, the United States Marines Maintenance Center, Farmer's Insurance, Coldwell Banker, National Seminars, the City of Glendale, Santa Clara Housing Authority, the Metropolitan Water District of Los Angeles, and the International House of Pancakes. A graduate of USC and Rutgers the State University, Gary taught English for many years at Rutgers and with the Los Angeles Community Colleges. His background also includes co-ownership of one of the first franchises of California Closets, and he is the author of numerous articles, columns, and reviews. He can be reached at *www.themouthtrap.com* or *www.thewritinginstitute.com*.